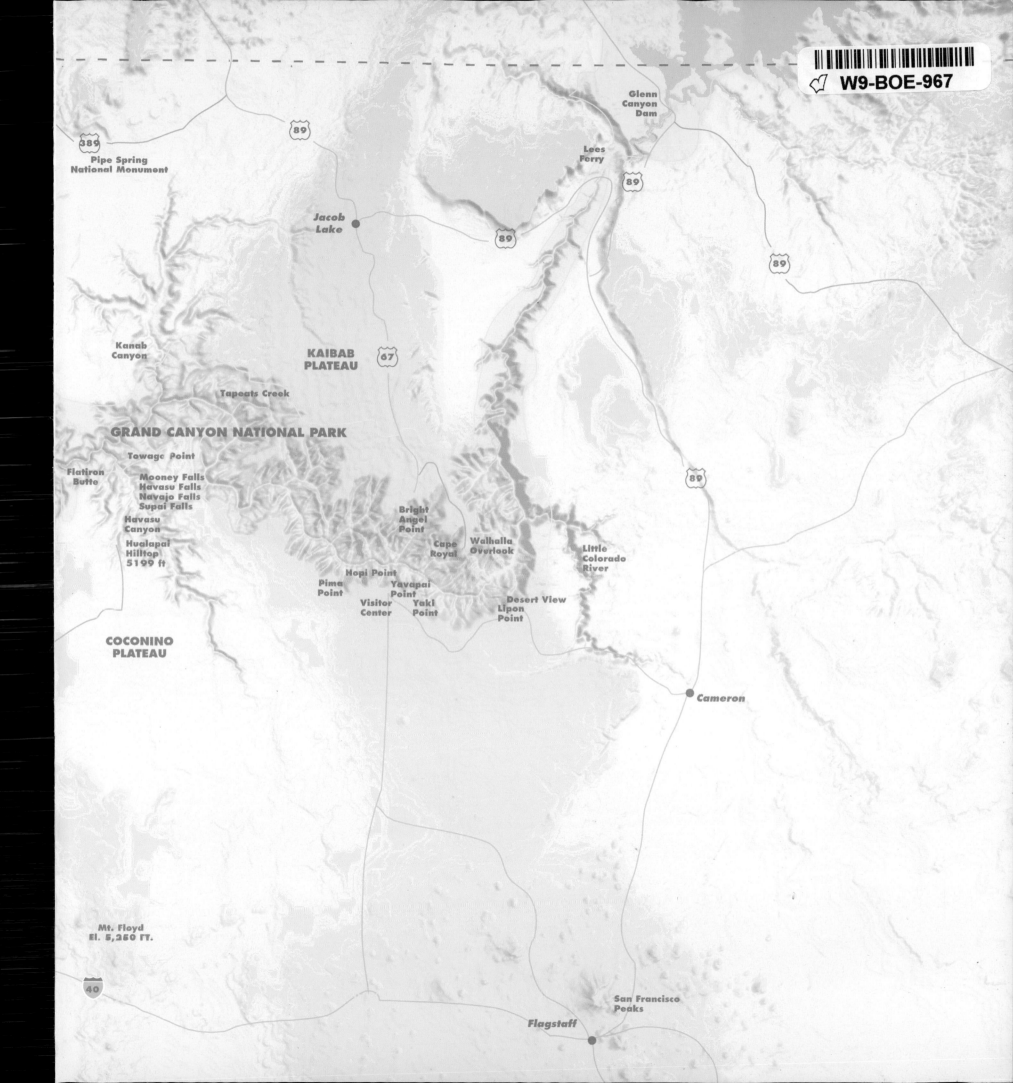

Glenn
Canyon
Dam

389
Pipe Spring
National Monument

89

Lees
Ferry

89

Jacob
Lake

89

89

Kanab
Canyon

KAIBAB
PLATEAU

67

Tapeats Creek

GRAND CANYON NATIONAL PARK

Towago Point

Flatiron
Butte

Mooney Falls
Havasu Falls
Navajo Falls
Supai Falls

Havasu
Canyon

Bright
Angel
Point

89

Hualapai
Hilltop
5199 ft

Cape
Royal

Walhalla
Overlook

Little
Colorado
River

Hopi Point

Pima
Point

Yavapai
Point

Visitor
Center

Yaki
Point

Desert View

Lipon
Point

COCONINO
PLATEAU

Cameron

Mt. Floyd
El. 5,260 FT.

40

San Francisco
Peaks

Flagstaff

"It has inspired ecstasy in photographers; it has moved poets and writers to absolute excesses of prose. There is, after all, nothing quite like this canyon anywhere else on the face of the earth."

PAGE STEGNER

GRAND

THE GRE

PAGE

PHOTOGRAPHY

HarperCollins**West** *A Division of HarperCollinsPublishers*

CANYON

AT ABYSS

STEGNER

BY JEFF GARTON

A Tehabi Book

DEDICATION

This book is dedicated to my wife, Lynn Stegner.

The Genesis Series was conceived by Tehabi Books and published by HarperCollins*West*. The series celebrates the epic geologic processes that created and continue to shape America's magnificent national parks and their distinctive ecosystems. Each book is written by one of the nation's most evocative nature writers and features images from some of the best nature photographers in the world.

Grand Canyon: The Great Abyss was produced by Tehabi Books. Susan Wels, *Genesis Series Editor*; Jeff Campbell, *Copy Editor*; Anne Hayes, *Copy Proofer*; Nancy Cash, *Managing Editor*; Andy Lewis, *Art Director*; Tom Lewis, *Editorial and Design Director*; Sharon Lewis, *Controller*; Chris Capen, *President*.

Written by Page Stegner, *Grand Canyon: The Great Abyss* features the photography of Jeff Garton. Supplemental photography was provided by Tom and Pat Leeson (pages 80, 83, 91) and Willard Clay (page 84). Technical, 3-D illustrations were produced by Sam Lewis. Source materials for the illustrations were provided as digital elevation models from the United States Geological Survey. Additional illustrations were produced by Andy Lewis and Tom Lewis.

For more information on the Grand Canyon, HarperCollins*West* and Tehabi Books encourage readers to contact the Grand Canyon Natural History Association at P.O. Box 399, Grand Canyon, AZ 86023; (602) 638-2481.

HarperCollins*West* and Tehabi Books, in association with The Basic Foundation, a not-for-profit organization whose primary mission is reforestation, will facilitate the planting of two trees for every one tree used in the manufacture of this book.

Library of Congress Cataloging-in-Publication Data
Stegner, Page.
   Grand Canyon : the great abyss / Page Stegner. — 1st ed.
        p. cm. — (Genesis Series)
   Includes index.
   ISBN 0-06-258573-8 (cloth). —
   ISBN 0-06-258564-9 (paperback).
   1. Grand Canyon (Ariz.) — Description and travel. 2. Grand Canyon
(Ariz.) — Pictorial works. 3. Natural history — Arizona — Grand
Canyon. 4. Natural history — Arizona — Grand Canyon — Pictorial works.
I. Title. II. Series: Genesis series
F788.S862 1995
917.91`320453—dc20   94-43220
                                           CIP

95 96 97 98 TBI 10 9 8 7 6 5 4 3 2 1

This edition is printed on acid-free paper that meets the American National Standards Institute Z39.48 Standard.

PAGE 1:

The view downriver from Toroweap.

PAGES 2-3:

Moonrise over the Palisades of the Desert.

PAGES 4-5:

Fog rises at Point Imperial.

PAGES 6-7:

The Esplanade as seen from Boysag Point.

TITLE PAGES 8-9:

Clouds over Marble Canyon.

THE GENESIS SERIES

GRAND CANYON

THE GREAT ABYSS

It has been praised as the most "sublime spectacle" in the world and condemned as the most "profitless locality" on earth. Some have peered into it with a sense of oppression and horror; others have been moved to great acts of creative expression and a sense of profound spiritual identification. It has inspired agony and ecstasy in thousands of photographers trying to deal with its changing light; it has moved poets and writers to absolute excesses of purple (and sometimes indecipherable) prose. There is, after all, nothing quite like this canyon anywhere else on the face of the earth.

Many of us, particularly those whose aesthetic sensibilities have been trained by pastoral hills, blue lakes, verdant meadows, and contented cows, don't quite know what to make of the Grand Canyon—at least not at first. I can think of nobody who put the problem more succinctly than Clarence Dutton, the man who led the first U.S. Geological Survey expedition into the region in 1880. "Great innovations," he said, "whether in art or literature, in science or in nature, seldom take the world by storm. They must be understood before they can be estimated, and must be cultivated before they can be understood."

So let's get some of the clinical factoids out of the way right up front. The Grand Canyon region extends, east to west, from the Echo Cliffs near Lees Ferry to the Grand Wash Cliffs near Lake Mead. On the north, it is bordered by the Kaibab, Kanab, Uinkaret, and Shivwits Plateaus, and on the south by the Coconino Plateau. The elevation of the North Rim at Grand Canyon Lodge is 8,200

The Little Colorado River Gorge, west of the Painted Desert.

REVELATION

feet; the South Rim at Grand Canyon Village is 6,965 feet. The highest juncture within the park boundaries is Point Imperial on the North Rim at 8,801 feet; Yaki Point on the South Rim is about fifteen hundred feet lower, at 7,262 feet.

The Colorado River drops ten thousand feet from its Green River headwaters in Wyoming's Wind River Range to its outlet in the Gulf of California (actually it never quite makes it all the way, dying in the sands of Laguna Salada a few miles short of the gulf). In total, it is about 1,700 miles long, and it is the drainage system for nearly 250,000 square miles—an area encompassing a significant portion of seven western states. Its Grand Canyon section, between Lees Ferry and the Grand Wash Cliffs, is 277 miles long—though the last 40 miles now lie beneath the waters of Lake Mead. The river through the canyon descends a total of 1,900 feet, or approximately 7.8 feet per mile. Its flow is controlled by Glen Canyon Dam and currently varies between a high of 20,000 cfs (cubic feet per second) and a low of 5,000 cfs. It carries a canyon-scouring sediment load of about 40,000 tons a day—a small fraction of its pre-dam burden of 380,000 to 500,000 tons per day.

The canyon area contained within the national park itself encompasses about nineteen hundred square miles. Its depth varies from less than a thousand feet downstream from Lees Ferry in the upper sections of Marble Canyon to six thousand at its deepest point in Granite Gorge. It varies in width from less than a mile to 17.5 miles from rim to rim.

Now that the data gods have been temporarily appeased, we can get more personal. I first encountered all of the above exactly fifty years ago. In 1944, after a six-year sojourn among the diminutive hills and hummocks of New England, my parents, both Westerners by nature and training, packed up their worldly possessions, tied them all on top of our Ford station wagon, and moved from Massachusetts to California. They took the southern route, old Highway 66, through St. Louis, Oklahoma City, across the Texas panhandle, and into New Mexico and Arizona.

I was six or seven at the time, and half a century has cleared my memory of much of that midsummer odyssey, though a few imagistic scraps and one king-sized revelation still remain. For scraps there is the overloaded, overheating Ford station wagon in which we motored sedately away from the lush greenery of the eastern United States and into the parched, uncharted wastelands beyond the hundredth meridian. There is a leaking canvas water bag that hung from the hood ornament, and a cylindrical "air cooler" that attached to the driver's seat window like a food tray at a drive-in restaurant. It failed to perform any cooling, though it did humidify—a particularly jolly feature through the damp heat of the East and Midwest.

For revelation there is . . . the revelation. That is what the British novelist J. B. Priestley called the Grand Canyon—"not a show place, a beauty spot, but a revelation," a place indescribable in "pigments or words." He said he had heard rumors that there were those who

From the Toroweap
Overlook above Lava
Falls, the canyon walls
drop precipitously three
thousand feet to the
Colorado River.

were disappointed by the spectacle, but he opined that such people would be disappointed by the Day of Judgment. "In fact," he mused, "the Grand Canyon is a sort of *landscape* Day of Judgment" (italics mine).

My revelation was somewhat different from the one experienced by Mr. Priestley, and perhaps it might be worth stepping back in time here for a moment to review it. I should like to film this retrospective from an elevated perspective, however. I no longer wish to be too closely identified with its author.

Let us imagine we are looking down into the rear seat of a Ford station wagon as it travels along Highway 66 east of Tucumcari, New Mexico, circa 1944. A snuffling preadolescent is expressing his lack of enthusiasm for cross-country expeditions in a tedious litany of toneless, monosyllabic questions: "Are we there yet? When are we gonna be there? How much farther?"

Trying to cheer the lout, his father begins to tell him fanciful tales about the wild and woolly West, promising encounters with cowboys and Indians, rattlesnakes, scorpions, Gila monsters, and the most horrible creature in the northern hemisphere, the "so terrible to look on it gives me the fantods just to think about" saber-toothed jackalope.

No response.

"This thing is all teeth and hair. It can run eighty miles an hour and jump forty feet in the air, and it devours side-hill cowgits in a single bite. Of course, the cowgit is somewhat at a disadvantage, what with its uphill legs being shorter and all—fine for grazing on steep slopes, but hell on flat ground."

"How far is it?"

"When we get to Arizona."

The desert rolls on, rises slowly to low juniper-pinyon woodland, then to pine forest as they climb toward the San Francisco Peaks. Dim recollection here of fry bread, or maybe a Navajo taco, then more desert, and father's voice saying, "Well, this is it, bub, jackalope country." Car stopping. Young Fauntleroy, groggy from his postprandial nap in the back seat, told to climb out. Peevishly complies. Is led stumbling across an asphalt parking lot past a sign announcing Yavapai Point. Hands placed on iron pipe railing at the edge of a rocky precipice. Where he stands blinking out across . . . the revelation.

Revelation? He sees flat rocks, red ledges, a void, an emptiness, nothing, an ensemble of dumb space and fractured horizons, hazy silence, collapsed perspectives. (I'm afraid we may have here one of those people about whom Mr. Priestley heard rumors.) He looks up and down, left and right, scans from rim to layered rim, begins to understand that he's been duped, bamboozled, bilked, gypped, swindled. He's been had. Sputtering disappointment, he turns and wails, "The jackalopes. Where are the jackalopes?"

Of Marble Gorge, John Wesley Powell wrote in 1869: "The Limestone of this canyon is often polished, and makes a beautiful marble. Sometimes the rocks are of many colors— white, grey, pink, and purple, with saffron tints."

PICTURED LEFT:

Early morning light burnishes the Kaibab limestone along the South Rim. The three-hundred-foot thick formation contains the fossil remains of more than eighty invertebrates, including brachiopods, corals, clams, mollusks, sea lilies, sponges, worms, and occasional fish teeth.

PICTURED RIGHT:

From Point Imperial, the view extends south across Marble Canyon and the Marble Platform toward the Painted Desert and the Kaibito Plateau. In the far distance, the Coconino Rim is visible just south of Desert View. In the foreground, a shaft of light strikes Mt. Hayden, a pinnacle of Coconino sandstone sitting on top of the Hermit shale and surrounded by typical Kaibab pine forest.

FOLLOWING PAGES:

In canyon country, tributary erosion often causes parts of the surrounding plateaus to erode away, forming isolated, broad-topped peaks called mesas. These continue eroding into narrow buttes—or temples, as they are frequently called in the Grand Canyon. In time, Vishnu Temple will be worn away into a mere remnant of a butte, such as the 250-million-year-old Duck Rock (foreground).

Across from Cape Royal, all the major formations from the Tonto Platform to the Coconino Plateau are clearly exposed on the cliff walls. The setting sun illuminates the Kaibab/Toroweap limestone on the canyon rim as well the Coconino sandstone below it. The sloping Bright Angel formation of the Tonto Platform is visible in the notch formed by Cape Royal on the near left and Vishnu Temple on the middle right. The San Francisco Peaks loom on the southern horizon.

Midday light at Tatahatso Point flattens the colors and contours of Marble Canyon below.

It has been about fifty years since this time-lapsed simulation, but I have to confess I still feel as if I'm looking for jackalopes when I stand on the rim of the Grand Canyon, staring out over a five-to-twelve-mile-wide gap, two hundred miles long and six thousand feet deep, with a river at the bottom the great environmentalist David Brower once described as the carotid artery of the intermountain West, and exposed rocks down there 1.7 billion years old. I possess the information. I understand that the geological history of the world is laid out before me. But it's too much. Really. I can't process it.

The truth is that a lot of people have trouble processing it—as any afternoon spent observing the sightseers at Yaki, Mather, Yavapai, and Hopi Points will demonstrate. Some simply have no information about what is out there in front of their eyes, and after a few obligatory snapshots for the folks back home, head for the snack bar. Others may simply find the spectacle unnerving. The southwestern writer Haniel Long said the Grand Canyon gave him a kind of "cosmic vertigo" and made him feel seasick and sleepless. Irvin Cobb of the *Saturday Evening Post* wrote, "You stand there gazing down the raw, red gullet of that great gosh-awful gorge, and you feel your self-importance shriveling up to nothing inside you." Even Clarence Dutton, the topographical engineer with the Powell survey in 1880, and a man who processed geological information better than almost anybody, used words like "awe," "dread," "shock," "oppression," "horror" to describe the initial sensation of gazing out over that sudden void, that saber-toothed jackalope of the mind.

We can only speculate what the first white men to encounter the Grand Canyon thought about their discovery. None of them got exactly lyrical. A group of Coronado's men under Don Garcia Lopez de Cardenas reached the South Rim in 1540, where they spent three days looking for a way to descend to the river. Unable to get more than a third of the way down, and depleted of their supply of water, they retraced their steps east to the Hopi villages from whence they had come. Having nothing remotely analogous in their experience against which to make comparisons, they reported that some of the rocks in the canyon were "bigger than the great tower of Seville."

Over two hundred years later, in 1776, Fray Francisco Garces, a Franciscan missionary and colleague of Juan Bautista de Anza, strayed into the region of the Aubrey Cliffs, where he met a band of Havasupai and spent an unsuccessful week trying to convert them at their village in Cataract Creek. Garces stolidly described the canyon as "profound" and remarked in his diary that he was "astonished by the roughness of this country, and at the barrier which nature has fixed therein." Beyond that, he seemed to have little to say. That same year the famous Dominguez/Escalante party, trying to return to Santa Fe from the Great Basin, wandered around lost for several weeks in a maze of side canyons before eventually discovering a way to cross the Colorado, near the present site of Lees Ferry. Escalante's account of this ordeal, like those of his predecessors, wastes little time in florid admiration of the scenery.

TOPOGRAPHY OF THE GRAND CANYON

The vastness of the Grand Canyon baffles our senses of size and dimension. As nature writer John C. Van Dyke wrote in *The Grand Canyon of the Colorado,* "The mind keeps groping for a scale of proportion—something whereby we can mentally measure. Standards of comparison break down and common experience helps us not at all . . . . The more one walks about the Canyon the vaster it becomes. Distance seems boundless."

The relief map on the following pages shows the configuration of the Grand Canyon as it cuts across the Kaibab Upwarp. At its western end, on the left side of the map, the blue-shaded area shows the upper reaches of Lake Mead, where the Colorado River is impounded by Hoover Dam after it emerges from the Grand Wash Cliffs. The Hualapai Indian Reservation occupies much of the territory to the south of the canyon, between the Grand Wash Cliffs and the river. On the opposite side of the canyon's western end is the Shivwits Plateau, dominated by the 6,990-foot mass of Mount Dellenbaugh.

The middle section of the map shows the Lower Granite Gorge portion of the Colorado River between Peach Springs Canyon (lower left) and Kanab Creek Canyon (upper right). The Hurricane Cliffs run north/south through the top center of the map on the stairsteplike ascent from the Shivwits to the Uinkaret Plateau. The great rift entering the main canyon from the south and cutting across the Coconino Plateau is Havasu Canyon, home to the

CROSS SECTION OF THE GRAND CANYON

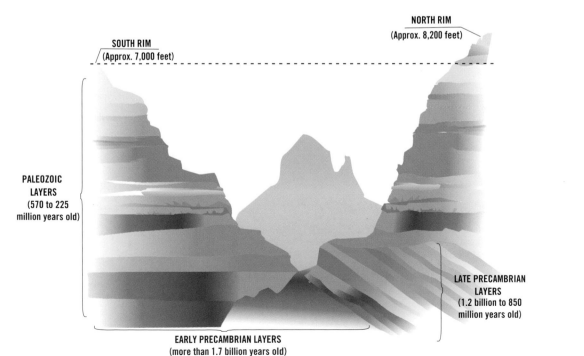

Erosion in the Grand Canyon has revealed layers of rock laid down over many geologic periods.

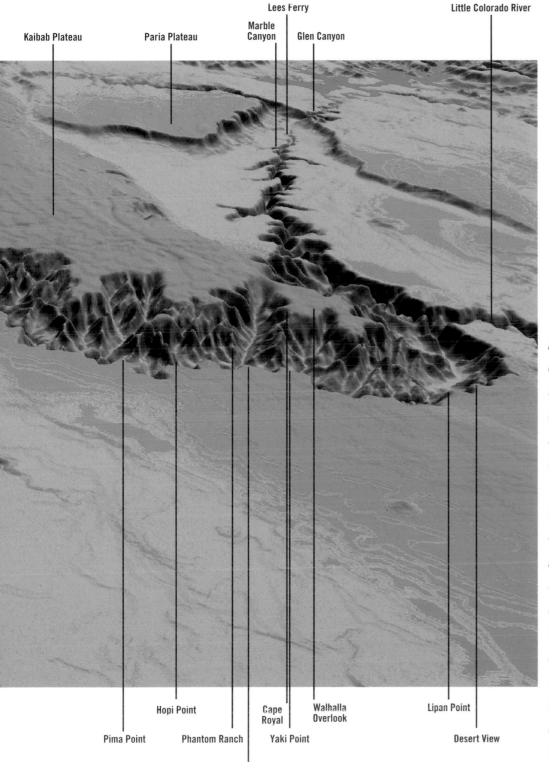

Kaibab Plateau

Paria Plateau

Marble Canyon

Lees Ferry

Glen Canyon

Little Colorado River

Pima Point

Hopi Point

Phantom Ranch

Cape Royal

Yaki Point

Walhalla Overlook

Lipan Point

Desert View

Grandview Point

Note: Although it may look like a photograph, this image is actually a computerized, extruded, topographic view. It was created using digital elevation models derived from the United States Geological Survey (USGS) satellite maps and traditional, flat USGS topography maps.

To prepare the extruded topo map, data from the USGS was downloaded from the Earth Science Information Center to a personal computer and converted into a three-dimensional model. There, a flat or "birds-eye" version was rendered which simulates a direct overhead view of the region (the end sheets on both inside covers of this book were reproduced from this version). The flat version was then tilted in order to create a view of the area from an angle 29 degrees off the horizon. Shadows, textures, and colors were added to represent a view that one might see from space.

J ust to the north of Havasu Canyon, Sinyala Butte rises a thousand feet above Sinyala Mesa.

And during the first half of the nineteenth century, there were a small number of Americans who penetrated the canyon region of southern Utah and northern Arizona—fur trappers like William Ashley and James Ohio Pattie and the Mormon colonizer Jacob Hamblin, who was sent out during the 1850s by Brigham Young to establish settlements at Moab, Lees Ferry, and St. George. But no systematic exploration of the canyon of the Colorado occurred until 1857, when the United States War Department ordered Lieutenant Joseph Christmas Ives to attempt to navigate the river from its mouth near Fort Yuma to the Mormon settlements in Utah. A fifty-eight-foot, steel-hulled steamboat was built in Philadelphia, dismantled and shipped around the horn to San Francisco, carried overland in wagons to the Gulf of California, and reassembled. On January 11, Ives and a company of twenty-four men departed Fort Yuma and steamed north in the newly christened *Explorer*. And immediately ran aground.

It was a bad omen. For the next 150 miles, the steamboat repeatedly encountered shoal waters, sunken rocks, and rapids. She ran aground a half dozen times and then finally suffered a horrendous wreck that flung everybody near the bow into the drink and nearly tore the stem clear out of the boat. Ives knew that he had gone as far by water as he was going to go, and if the mission was to succeed, it would have to continue on foot.

The company marched north and then east as far as Cataract Canyon (now called Havasu) and the village of the Havasupai Indians—a point that on today's maps would lie roughly midway between Lake Mead and Lake Powell and nearly opposite the great canyon of Kanab Creek. Ives mistakenly identified Kanab Canyon as the main branch of the Colorado and, being unable to cross the river and venture into it, decided he had now gone on *foot* as far as he was going to go, and turned back.

Not that this seemed to make him all that unhappy. From the tone of voice evident in his 1861 *Report Upon the Colorado River of the West*, Lieutenant Ives appears to have seen enough: "The region last explored is, of course, altogether valueless. It can be approached only from the south, and after entering it there is nothing to do but to leave. Ours has been the first, and will doubtless be the last, party of whites to visit this profitless locality. It seems intended by nature that the Colorado river, along the greater portion of its lonely and majestic way, shall be forever unvisited and undisturbed."

As a lot of people have observed, Ives was a lousy prophet. In 1993, nearly five million people visited the two rims of the Grand Canyon, and over a million actually ventured down into it either by mule or shank's mare. Twenty thousand people floated the river on rafting trips. Another eight hundred thousand viewed the park from one of the nonstop "scenic air tours" (primarily helicopter over-flights) that rattle the canyon's solitude more than 70 percent of the time. In fact, Grand Canyon Airport is the busiest airport in Arizona, except for Phoenix, and daytime conversations in Tusayan are conducted in short bursts between the racket of helicopter departures and landings.

During the summer months, up to six thousand cars a day were observed endlessly circling Grand Canyon Village, fighting for fewer than twenty-five hundred parking spaces, and over a hundred bus tours a day, on average, rolled through the park. *The Colorado Plateau Advocate*, a publication of the conservation organization the Grand Canyon Trust, observed that during July of 1993 "more than 231,000 vehicles carried 800,000 people into the park. Another 14,000 visitors arrived by train, and approximately 30,000 people roared over the canyon in 10,000 separate air tours."

The "profitless locality" is not only massively visited, it is massively impacted and disrupted in other critical ways, the most obvious of these being air pollution. Smog from Phoenix, Los Angeles, and the coal-fired power plants at Page, Arizona, and Four Corners, New Mexico, cuts visibility by an annual average of 30 percent. And, during the winter, a pale, sulfate haze propagated by the Navajo Generating Station at Page, a hundred miles north of park headquarters, can wash out the view by as much as 70 percent. Navajo spews an average of 240 tons of sulfur dioxide a day into the southwestern atmosphere, though it has agreed to clean up its act by 1999 and reduce that amount to 24 tons.

But the major challenge that the National Park Service (NPS) faces today at Grand Canyon is how to manage a volume of visitors that already vastly exceeds the park's infrastructure, and that is projected to increase by the year 2000 to seven million annual visitations. As far back as 1978, then-Superintendent Merle Stitt acknowledged that the NPS mandate to manage the parks "by such a means as will leave them unimpaired for the enjoyment of future generations" was an unattainable goal at Grand Canyon. He simply did not have the staff or the budget to do it. And in 1978 Stitt was only trying to accommodate three million visitors.

It is hoped that the updated Grand Canyon General Management Plan will seriously address the need for establishing limits. The time has come. Obviously there is a real need to restrict private automobile access to the South Rim in general and to continue to develop shuttle bus transit along East and West Rim roads. We are, as historian Roderick Nash and others have long argued, loving our parks and wild areas to death. The biggest threat to wilderness used to be from grazing, mining, and timber harvesting; now it's from what one cynical wag referred to as industrial-strength tourism.

Perhaps there is no solution to this phenomenon, short of wrapping the whole Kaibab Upwarp in concertina wire and running people off with packs of rabid dogs. Or perhaps the solution is very simple. We stop the tour buses twenty miles short of the rim and usher people into a warehouse-size cinema, where they'll have a quick and easy virtual reality tour of the park. In fact, the prototype is already in place in Tusayan, where the IMAX Theater presents, in six-track Dolby and on a screen seventy feet high, *Grand Canyon—The Hidden Secrets*. We won't close the canyon—we'll just insist that anybody who wants to see the real McCoy walks. Like Cardenas, Father Garces, Dominguez and Escalante, and Lieutenant Joseph Christmas Ives.

A *view of Marble Canyon from Buck Farm Canyon Overlook.*

From Yaki Point, it is a
4,700-foot drop in
elevation to the river
and a 6.3-mile descent
along the South Kaibab
Trail.

For the eleven miles between North Canyon and South Canyon, the Colorado follows an almost straight path. Rafters encounter nearly one midsize rapid per mile along that stretch of river because of numerous washes that enter the canyon from the eastern rim of the Marble Platform.

A view of the Unkar Creek drainage from Walhalla Overlook. Here, the Colorado turns ninety degrees and flows from Marble Canyon into the Upper Granite Gorge of the Grand Canyon.

Let's once again briefly address the literal-minded laity who like to have a program before they sign up for the tour. Take an ordinary road map, a ruler, and a pen. Using the Utah/Arizona border as a northern boundary, and the Arizona/Nevada border as a western boundary, extend the western boundary in a straight line south to Interstate 40, then draw a straight line east to Flagstaff, and another line north to Page. What has been enclosed in this square of about 150 miles on a side is the southwestern section of the Colorado Plateau.

While the general region contains much of the Coconino Plateau to the south, and a series of staircase plateaus to the north (the Kaibab, Kanab, Uinkaret, and Shivwits), the word *plateau* conjures up the wrong image. "Plateau" implies that the cocktail lounge at Grand Canyon Lodge on the North Rim is at the same elevation as its counterpart in the El Tovar Hotel on the South Rim, and it's not. It's a thousand feet higher. So let's forget "plateau." Bulge, boil, blister, or bunion is a more appropriate metaphor, though there may be consensus that "Colorado Blister" and "Kaibab Bunion" are not exactly lyrical.

The explanation for this humping-up effect has long been debated and has variously been described as a consequence of disparate forces—vulcanism, continental drift, and isostasy (the

Cliffs of Coconino sandstone. "All day long we had seen in the magnificent walls besides caverns and galleries resemblances to every form of architectural design, turrets, forts, balconies, castles, and a thousand strange and fantastic suggestions . . ."

—Frederick Dellenbaugh, Second Powell Expedition, 1871 72.

SILTS, GRITS, AND GRAVELS

theory that tells us if you push down over here, something will pop up over there). The subduction of the Pacific plate beneath the western edge of the North American plate may have had something to do with the uplifting of the entire Colorado Plateau, though the theory is unproven. Geologists currently concerned with the uplifting of the Colorado Plateau think it may have been caused not by erosion-induced isostatic pressure, but by changes in the density of the earth's crust. Dense mantle rock becomes converted into thicker and lighter crustal rock. Since crustal rock floats on the earth's mantle, the thicker it gets, the higher it floats. Voilà—uplift.

But whatever the explanation, as far back as sixty-five million years ago, or so some geologists have argued, volcanic pressures beneath the southern province of the plateau were already causing it to swell upward in a broad dome, with the Ancestral Colorado River flowing along its eastern boundary. There was no Grand Canyon, of course. Radiometric dating of riverbed deposits show that the Colorado River began carving the Grand Canyon relatively recently—about five and a half million years ago—and completed the job (to its present depth) a little over a million years ago. Only yesterday.

One of the biggest debates has long been over this question: Since water can't run uphill, *how* did the Colorado River manage to carve a 227-mile-long drainage ditch, six thousand feet deep, across the middle of a bunion? Of course, there are those, like the Cracked Earth Society, who have argued that it didn't, that the uplifting of the region was similar to a cake rising too fast and splitting apart. The Cracked Earth Society does not enjoy a large membership these days. Neither does the group asserting the "hand of God" theory, nor the "hand of man" advocates, who shrug and say, "We dug the Panama Canal; we could'a dug the Grand Canyon too."

John Wesley Powell, the first man to systematically explore the canyons of the Colorado, believed that the river was there in its existing course *before* uplifting began (sixty-five million years ago) and merely cut more deeply into its channel as the land rose. Unfortunately, as mentioned, the geological evidence disputes this. Radiometric dating of the Muddy Creek formation underlying river deposits at the western end of the canyon, near the Grand Wash Cliffs, indicate the formation is only about six million years old. The Colorado River deposits on top of it, therefore, have to be younger. So Powell's explanation does not compute—though to give him his due, he did not have radioactive isotopes to help with his calculations.

There have been other hypotheses, but the theory that until a few years ago seemed to have the most currency was the two-river theory, postulated by a group of geologists convened by Edwin McKee at a 1964 symposium. On the eastern side of the Kaibab Upwarp, the argument went—where evidence shows the Ancestral Colorado to be thirty-seven million years old—the river ran more or less as it does today. There was one major difference, however: where it now meets the Little Colorado and abruptly changes direction from north/south to east/west, there was no turn—and no Little Colorado. The ancestral river simply continued south along the course of what, millions of years later (and flowing in the opposite direction), would *become* the

After a rain- or snowstorm, the canyon is often shrouded in clouds that billow up from the superheated depths below. Here fog streaks the light above Nankoweap Canyon and the eastern wall of the Marble Platform, called Desert Facade.

Little Colorado. Eventually, it dumped itself into a great lake called Bidahochi.

At the same time, a second river system, the Hualapai, was cutting, cutting, cutting into the western flank of the Kaibab Upwarp in what is known as headward erosion (a stream that keeps eating backward from its point of origin). In time (about five million years) it chewed its way completely eastward until it broke through the last remaining veil of rock . . . and captured the poor old Ancestral Colorado, dawdling along on its way down to Bidahochi.

It must have been madness. It must have been a parting of the stone and a sudden meeting of the waters. Roil and chaos, riot and pandemonium. Two great rivers abruptly meeting; the Hualapai (being lower at its outlet) abducting the Ancestral Colorado and causing it to suddenly reverse its course. The inlet to Lake Bidahochi becomes an outlet, prehistoric rafting trips heading for the Painted Desert Marina and Boatell are sucked backward as the river stops abruptly, backs up, and begins to flow west rather than south. Head boatmen make a quick itinerary change; promise all their passengers a steak dinner and a mule ride out at Phantom Ranch. Before they really get into deep schist down in the gorge.

Unfortunately, the two-rivers theory has as many problems as the hyperbolic description above. Alluvial gravel deposits covered by a lava flow have been found on both the north *and* south sides of what is now the Grand Canyon, and radiometric dating has shown them to be about six million years old. The deposits are clearly from the same source. Since neither an alluvial gravel fan nor a basaltic flow covering it can cross a canyon (just as water can't run uphill), the only reasonable conclusion is that the canyon wasn't there six million years ago. And if it wasn't there, then the river that didn't cut it wasn't there either.

So where was it? As an undergraduate I flunked geology. I now understand why. On the other hand, I didn't do so well in theology either. But unless we're just going to throw in the towel and go for the "hand of God" explanation, we'd better look at the latest hypothesis, which will no doubt soon be modified or out of date. It's the "racetrack valley" theory, and without getting into it in any but the most superficial way, it argues that the Ancestral Colorado River circumnavigated the Kaibab Upwarp in what is called a racetrack valley and flowed off (nobody knows where) to the northwest.

It seems doubtful that an Ancestral Colorado actually existed when the Kaibab Plateau started uplifting during the Laramide Orogeny—a mountain-building period that began around eighty million years ago and went on for forty million years (creating the modern Rocky Mountains in the process and helping to isolate the Colorado Plateau). But when it did come into being, the Kaibab Upwarp was certainly in place, and the river had to flow around it along a trough carved through soft stone sandwiched between two harder sections of rock. At what is now the Grandview Monocline (just past Grandview Point, at the eastern edge of the Kaibab Upwarp), between two uplifting folds of hard Kaibab limestone, the river turned and started cutting westward through softer rock, bisecting the Kaibab Upwarp and excavating in the process the Upper, Middle, and Lower Granite Gorges of the Grand Canyon.

A *view of cascades such as Upper Deer Creek Falls inspired John Wesley Powell's journal entry of August 23, 1869:*

"*. . .we pass a stream on the right, which leaps into the Colorado by a direct fall of more than a hundred feet, forming a beautiful cascade . . . the stream pours through a narrow crevice above into a deep pool below. Around on the rocks, in the cave-like chamber, are set beautiful ferns, with delicate fronds and enameled stalks.*"

LAYERS OF TIME

Coming upon the Grand Canyon for the first or the fiftieth time, one's initial sensation is likely to be awe. As Clarence Dutton wrote in 1882, "A perpetual glamour envelopes the landscape. Things are not what they seem and the perceptions cannot tell us what they are . . . . It is never the same, even from day to day to day, or even hour to hour. Every passing cloud, every change in the position of the sun, recasts the whole."

But spend enough time peering into the abyss, and eventually curiosity replaces amazement. Just what is it that makes up the tone and temper of that incredible landscape? What are all those layers and ledges?

The 1.7- to 2-billion-year-old rocks at the bottom of the Inner Gorge are the oldest exposed rocks in the Grand Canyon. They are, in fact, believed to be the roots of ancient alps that once rose fifteen to twenty thousand feet over the region. These ancient, granitic rocks—technically identified as the Vishnu Metamorphic Complex and Zoroaster Plutonic Complex—were formed (or reformed) under great heat and pressure during periods of

STRATIGRAPHIC PROFILES

GRAND CANYON FORMATIONS **GEOLOGIC PERIOD**

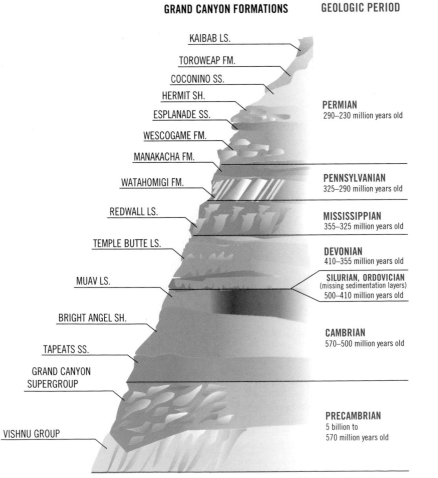

KAIBAB LS.

TOROWEAP FM.

COCONINO SS.

HERMIT SH.

PERMIAN
290–230 million years old

ESPLANADE SS.

WESCOGAME FM.

MANAKACHA FM.

PENNSYLVANIAN
325–290 million years old

WATAHOMIGI FM.

REDWALL LS.

MISSISSIPPIAN
355–325 million years old

TEMPLE BUTTE LS.

DEVONIAN
410–355 million years old

SILURIAN, ORDOVICIAN
(missing sedimentation layers)
500–410 million years old

MUAV LS.

BRIGHT ANGEL SH.

CAMBRIAN
570–500 million years old

TAPEATS SS.

GRAND CANYON
SUPERGROUP

PRECAMBRIAN
5 billion to
570 million years old

VISHNU GROUP

FM. = Formation., SS. = Sandstone., SH. = Shale., LS. = Limestone.,

This chart shows the chronological layering of the Grand Canyon's geologic formations.

At the very bottom of the pile, in the deep gloom of the Inner Gorge, is the Vishnu schist and Zoroaster granite of the Precambrian era.

Tonto Platform. Above the Tapeats lies the broad, sloping shelf of Bright Angel shale. This layer grades, in turn, into the eroding cliffs and ledges of Muav limestone.

As the eye rises to the canyon's rim, the most easily recognizable formations are the massive red cliffs of Redwall limestone that form a distinctive band about midway between the Tonto Platform and the rim. Equally distinctive is the band of yellow Coconino sandstone about five hundred feet below the rim. The topmost layer, which comprises the surface of both the Kaibab Plateau on the north side of the Grand Canyon and the Coconino Plateau on the south, is a bed of three-hundred-foot-thick Kaibab limestone.

In this panorama one can see all these major stratigraphic features of the Grand Canyon, with the exception of the Grand Canyon Supergroup. The view from Yaki Point shown here is easterly, across the canyon toward the Walhalla Plateau. The butte at the far right is Vishnu Temple, and the flat mesa next to it is Wotans Throne. Cape Royal is visible at the upper right-hand corner of the center section.

A wall of the Vishnu schist at the bottom of Trinity Canyon.

*I*n Blacktail Canyon, 600-million-year-old Tapeats sandstone (top) sits directly on top of 1.2-billion- to 850-million-year-old rock. The more than 200 million years of deposits that have vanished between these two formations were lost to erosion. The resulting missing link in the geological record is called the Great Unconformity.

*L*ayered rock formations at Toroweap.

DESERT VARNISH

The dark brown to black patina that one commonly sees staining cliff faces in canyon country is the result of iron and manganese oxides washed out of the soil from the plateau above and dissolved in a solution of rainwater. Over a period of many hundreds of years it discolors the rocks beneath as the rainwater flows downward. It is not uncommon to see the true color of the subsurface rock on a cliff coated with desert varnish—generally tan- or buff-colored patches where a slab has fallen away. In the Grand Canyon, the most distinctive layer from river to rim is the five-hundred-foot-thick band of Redwall limestone. Made up of dolomite, chert, and limestone, the Redwall is essentially gray in color—except that its surface has been stained by iron oxide leaching out of the overlying Supai Group. This is not desert varnish, but the principle is the same.

Near Desert View, a few miles in from the eastern entrance to the park, there is an overlook called Lipan Point. It is more or less directly above the place where the Colorado turns forty-five degrees and starts flowing across the Kaibab toward Nevada instead of south through the Painted Desert toward Phoenix. One can look down not only on this radical bend but north into Marble Canyon and west along the Tonto Plateau and the precipice above Upper Granite Gorge, as well as into the gorge itself. The canyon rims (north and south) are equally exposed from this vantage and create a near-seamless horizon between earth and sky.

A great many more people visit Desert View at Navajo Point a few miles down the road, largely because it has a whole host of visitor's services—including a store where you can buy the ubiquitous T-shirts and faux Indian crafts. But Lipan Point provides the best panoramic view in this part of the park. To the northeast, you can look out fifty miles over the canyon to the Vermillion and Echo Cliffs, and another forty or fifty miles beyond that to Navajo Mountain; to the northwest, the formations that lie in the far distance are Cape Royal, Vishnu Temple, Wotans Throne, Zoroaster, Isis, and Shiva Temples, and for all I know the Powell Plateau. Red ledges. Revelation. Mr. Priestley's landscape Day of Judgment. No wonder Clarence Dutton, who gave title to many of the formations in the canyon, thought they should be named after gods, not men.

From rim to river the eye descends, layer by layer, through 1.7 billion years of geological time. Across the chasm, and just at the foot of Apollo Temple, there is one of the best displays of what is called the Great Unconformity (an unconformity is a physical gap in the geological record). Six-hundred-million-year-old rocks lie directly on top of 1.2-billion- to 850-million-year-old rocks (known as the Grand Canyon Supergroup), which, in turn, lie directly on top of 1.7-billion-year-old rocks. To put it another way, there is a blank space in the geological account out there of more than 200 million years, and another blank space of about 500 million years.

The river curves around below that great, soft-looking slope of limestone, shale, quartzite, and siltstone, all stained a deep purple with iron oxide. To the west, it tucks behind a long, obscuring butte of Redwall limestone and then appears once again, briefly, in the Upper Granite Gorge below Hance Creek and Hance Creek Rapid.

Seventeen-hundred-million-year-old rock? That is a span of eternity which is completely meaningless, like the information that the earth itself is 4.5 billion years old, or that there are, on average, 100 billion solar masses in a galaxy, or that light traveling in a vacuum for a year covers 9.46 trillion kilometers. Unimaginable. Unthinkable. Preposterous.

Nevertheless, to accommodate those of us of limited intelligence, there have been numerous attempts to conceptualize geological time as it is represented in the Grand Canyon rocks—ancient rocks in what seems unarguably to be a very young canyon. One favored gambit is to represent on a twenty-four-hour clock the interval of time between the actual formation of the rock (schist) exposed at the bottom of the Inner Gorge and the beginning of the Colorado River's canyon cutting. In this scheme the world (4.5 billion years old) is formed just after 12:00 A.M., and the schist (1.7 billion years old) in the early afternoon. The river starts carving the canyon (5.5 million years old) at 11:58 P.M. Human life begins at 11:59 P.M.; your personal tenure on earth, dear reader (and mine, assuming we both live very long lives), passes by in less than half a second. None of this is of much comfort as we stand there at Lipan Point trying to assimilate what we're looking at, but it may give us a clue as to why we're feeling so queasy and insignificant.

If you don't know where you are, poet and writer Wendell Berry has reminded us, it's difficult to know who you are. To which we might add, in the canyonlands of southern Utah and northern Arizona, it's hard to know where you are unless you know where you would have been if you'd been around a couple billion years ago. It's very weird out there. It requires explanation. And explanations require not only information but leaps of faith and lots of imagination.

We can stand at almost any elevated point along the 10,700 square miles encompassing the Grand Canyon and try to begin to comprehend our surroundings. The first step is to ignore the fact that we are peering between our wingtips into an appalling, mile-deep gorge and imagine that we are standing on the flat floor of an enormous, ancient seabed, a vast plain of lava and sedimentary deposits. We'll have to take the geologists' word for it that through compression, chemistry, and time, all the loose, drifty detritus around us gets turned into solid rock. Now, in our mind's eye, we move the earth's crust underneath all this rock so that eventually it breaks apart in fault blocks and gets thrust up into high, snow-capped mountains. We imagine more heat and pressure, and turn the bottom-most deposits underneath the mountains into a metamorphic rock called schist; then we bring on the eroding agents of wind, ice, and rain. We do this for three to four hundred million years, until everything but that base of schist is worn away and we are back standing once more on our flat plain.

Now repeat the above—except, for the next phase of geologic history, let's make the sedimentary deposits over two and a half miles thick and begin to sprinkle in some unicellular algae, nautiloids, ammonoids, trilobites, and little bony fish. And, of course, we make the seas advance and retreat, advance and retreat. During the intervals of retreat, we'll lay down a lot of nonmarine deposits like river silt and blowing sand. Move the earth's crust again, fracture and tilt the surface, create another range of fault-block mountains, erode them away. No hurry about all this. In fact, we've got millions of years to get the job done.

Perhaps it's enough just to conserve the essential information and forget trying to imagine the scene. We need only remind ourselves that as we stand there at Lipan Point gazing at the panorama spread out before us, we are looking at what are, in effect, the geological tree rings from the two oldest geological eras, ranging from 2 billion to 225 million years old.

At the very bottom of the pile, in the deep gloom of the Inner Gorge, there is the Vishnu schist and Zoroaster granite of the earliest period in geologic time. About two billion years ago, sand, silt, mud, and clay began accumulating at the bottom of a Precambrian sea, eventually attaining a depth of nearly ten miles. When the region underwent a period of mountain-building

Many of the buttes in the Grand Canyon were named for exotic deities by Clarence Dutton, chief geologist with the Powell Survey and the first man to conduct a study of its geological history. Dutton found formations like Vishnu Temple much too sublime to be given common, unexalted titles.

upheaval about 1.7 billion years ago, these sedimentary layers of shale, limestone, and sandstone were infused by liquid magma from beneath the earth's crust. Under great heat and pressure, both igneous and sedimentary rocks were metamorphosed into the schist and gneiss we now find exposed, and though it may be hard to imagine, many geologists believe that there was a range of alpine peaks where there is now a "dreadful abyss." These black, cheerless rocks of Upper, Middle, and Lower Granite Gorges are, in fact, the remnant roots of a once-towering mountain range.

Above the schist lie scattered outcroppings of 1.2-billion- to 850-million-year-old basalts, limestones, sandstones, and shales known as the Grand Canyon Supergroup (which includes the Chuar and Unkar Groups, some of which are displayed across the floor of the canyon below Lipan Point). Fossils of marine algae, raindrops, cross-bedding, mud cracks, and ripple marks indicate that these rocks were formed during a time of alternating marine and coastal environments. Evidence suggests that about 850 million years ago, they too were subjected to uplifting—yet another mountain range formed on the eroded remnants of its predecessor. And then, those peaks, too, were worn down and washed away. As mentioned, there is a gap in the geological record (the Great Unconformity) that spans anywhere from 280 million to 830 million years, and what exactly happened during this tedious intermission is largely a matter of deduction and reasoned conjecture. Whatever happened, all but the schist, gneiss, and the Grand Canyon Supergroup has eroded away.

It isn't until about 570 million years ago that the register resumes in the rocks that rest on top of the Grand Canyon Supergroup—the Tapeats sandstone, Bright Angel shale, Muav and Temple Butte limestone, Redwall limestone, Supai Group, Hermit shale, Coconino sandstone, Toroweap formation, and finally, the Kaibab formation that comprises the rimrock on both sides of the canyon. It is a many-layered cake, and during a dozen visits to the canyon over nearly as many years I have tried assiduously to memorize the order of this stack. Then one day it occurred to me that this just wasn't information that was going to stick, and I happily gave it up. If I need to know, there are a dozen reference books that will solve my problem.

There are, however, a few distinctive features that even the C– student can't forget if he wishes to locate himself on a visual ascent from river to rim. The ancient Vishnu schist of the Inner Gorge is impossible to forget. It's nearly black, and if you're down there on the river floating past it, it gives you the creeps. The broad benchland called the Tonto Plateau just above the Inner Gorge consists of a dark brown sandstone called Tapeats, which gives way, as one moves back from the gorge, to a slope of greenish, Bright Angel shale. Both are easy to recognize topographically. And about midway up the canyon walls, the sheer, five- to six-hundred-foot cliff that is visible throughout the Grand Canyon is Redwall limestone, impossible to mistake because it is so massive and so . . . red, stained that color by the formations above it. The whitish or cream-colored cap that forms the rim of this entire aggregation is Kaibab limestone. You can't mistake it because there isn't anything above it.

The Supai Group is a geologic formation of shale and limestone capped by three layers of sandstone. Six hundred feet thick, and overlain by three hundred feet of deep red Hermit shale, it is responsible for the color of the massive cliffs of Redwall limestone so prominent throughout the Grand Canyon.

A *view of the Sinking Ship formation from an overlook near Grandview Point.*

*S*umner Butte was
named in honor of John
Colton (Jack) Sumner, a
Colorado mountaineer
and trading post opera-
tor who accompanied
Powell during his 1869
exploration of the
Colorado River. Sumner,
in fact, claimed in his
diary to have suggested
the idea of the expedi-
tion to Powell, although
no other sources verify
his assertion.

And what happened to all the Mesozoic formations that used to lie on top of the Kaibab—the Moenkopi, Shinarump, Chinle, Moenave, Kayenta, Navajo, Carmel, Dakota, Tropic, Wahweap, Kaiparowits, and Wasatch? Simple. Everything laid down within the last 225 million years has been almost entirely eroded away in the Grand Canyon area and can only be found above Marble Canyon—in the Echo and Vermillion Cliffs and at Cedar Mountain and Red Butte near the South Rim. Twelve formations along with twelve known unconformities gone down the river. That's a lot of silt, and a lot of scouring power.

Which accounts, in no small measure, for the depth and profile of the Grand Canyon we look at today. The stairstep formation of its walls has largely to do with the hardness or softness of the exposed layers (put simply, hard rock forms sheer cliffs, soft rock forms benches and slopes). But far more intriguing is how that little dinky river down there carved such an enormous cavity in the earth. After all, in terms of water volume, the Colorado is one-thirtieth the size of the Mississippi, and there's no Grand Canyon in Iowa.

At the risk of oversimplifying, the river had help from wind and weather. Water (in the form of rain and frost) seeps into the porous sandstones, limestones, and shales, breaking them down and dissolving their bonding particles. During the winter months, ice forming in cracks and fissures wedges stone apart, weakening large blocks and slabs and attenuating their adherence to the main cliff. Wind plays a minor, though relentless, role in blowing things around and weakening substructures. Earthquakes occasionally remodel the turf in major and momentous ways. Plants gain a toehold in a pocket of soil, and their root systems perform the same chiseling, prying, crevice-cracking service as the ice. Hot days, cold nights. Constant expansion and contraction. Whatever the specifics, the end result over time is that everything that is vertical winds up horizontal. The perpendicular gets undermined and weakened, softer formations become unable to support overlying strata, land slides and rock falls bring it all down. The world wants desperately to be flat. Given enough time, it will be.

And, of course, this weathering process continues relentlessly, not only along the Colorado River corridor but in its tributary canyons as well. Melting snows from the Kaibab Plateau, as well as flash floods caused by torrential summer rains, wash it all down, scrubbing every gulch, gorge, fissure, and ravine along the way, deepening them, chewing away at their margins, and dumping a tremendous amount of grit and grind into the daily flow of the main river.

Indeed, before the building of Glen Canyon Dam and the consequent formation of that great silt pond, Lake Powell, the Colorado carried enough abrasive material in a day to fill about four thousand dump trucks every hour. Which turned the little river into the cosmic Chore Boy. Today its silt load has been reduced to less than a fifth of the grit it transported during its undammed, untamed days. And that change, in turn, has affected the nature of the flora and fauna that inhabit its riparian corridor.

Between 225 and 65 million years ago, anywhere from four thousand to eight thousand feet of sandstone and shale deposits were laid down over the Colorado Plateau. Near the Grand Canyon, all of these deposits have been eroded away, except in two places—here at Cedar Mountain, located at the eastern boundary of the park, and at Red Butte, between Tusayan and Valle.

In the distance, the rock strata tilting down toward the river display a clear example of the Great Unconformity. The granite foundation beneath the angled formations is 1.7 billion years old, while the layer on top of it—called the Grand Canyon Supergroup—is 1.2 billion to 850 million years old. Half a billion years of geologic history have eroded away in between them.

ANCIENT MOUNTAINS

During the first decade of the twentieth century, John Muir visited the Grand Canyon. Of his first impressions, he wrote: "In a dry, hot monotonous forested plateau, seemingly boundless, you come suddenly and without warning upon the edge of a gigantic and sunken landscape of the wildest, most multitudinous features, and those features, sharp and angular, are made of flat beds of limestone and sandstone forming a spiry, jagged, gloriously colored mountain-range countersunk in a level gray plain."

Muir's vision was percipient. Based on the folding of the metamorphic and igneous rocks in the Granite Gorge portion of the Grand Canyon, there is considerable evidence that these 1.7- to 2-billion-year-old schists and gneisses were the foundation of a range of Alp-like mountains, fifteen to twenty thousand feet high, that occupied

Walls of schist, possibly the roots of ancient mountains, along the Colorado river in Granite Gorge.

Once mountains have been formed, they are gradually worn down by the process of erosion—which is the answer to the question, "What happened to all these alleged alpine peaks that once stood where the Grand Canyon is today?" The key ingredient in erosion is water. Whether in the form of snow, rain, or glacial ice—which is a relatively speedy erosional force—water, in addition to wind and chemical weathering, tore down the mighty peaks. The same force that carved the mile-deep canyon where the lofty mountains once stood eventually tore them down.

ROCKY MOUNTAINS
14,000 ft.

RIO GRANDE   MANZANO MOUNTAINS

GREAT PLAINS

When one is day-hiking in the Grand Canyon, it is possible to get the impression that there isn't much out there in the way of animal life—nothing but lizards, ravens, and the abominable *Humanus mucosus*, also known as the great-nosed sightseer. In small part, this is because few of us are actually in the habit of seeing what we look at; in large part, it is because a significant percentage of the animal life that is, in fact, out there is nocturnal. Nothing with an IQ higher than a chuckwalla is going to hang out in the furnace glow of a midsummer afternoon on the South Rim, or the Tonto Platform, or the river corridor. The maximum mean daily temperature at Phantom Ranch in July is 106 degrees; in the Inner Gorge it can often reach over 115.

The Grand Canyon region actually harbors a huge variety of life—70 species of mammals, 280 species of birds (of which 40 are year-round residents), 44 species of amphibians and reptiles, 7 species of fish, and at least 2 species of the *Humanus mucosus*. Neither of these —the hairy-pated nor the follically impaired—are vulnerable to predation, and they are, as noted elsewhere, increasing in numbers that will ultimately devastate the remnants of an already compromised habitat.

THE SCORPION AND THE KAIBAB SQUIRREL

The great diversity of life in the Grand Canyon is a consequence of the broad spectrum of ecological zones contained within its boundaries, zones that are basically defined by altitude, geology, and climatic conditions.

The concept of "life zones" was first articulated in the late nineteenth century by Dr. C. Hart Merriam, director of the Division of Ornithology and Mammology for the U.S. Department of Agriculture. Merriam divided North America into seven major vegetation belts, which he identified as Tropical, Lower Sonoran, Upper Sonoran, Transition, Canadian, Hudsonian, and Arctic-Alpine—and he argued that a thousand-foot change in altitude is biologically equivalent to a three-hundred-mile latitudinal journey at sea level. When Merriam's work was conducted, the incredible complexity of influences on the distribution of plants and animals was only beginning to be understood, and the interrelationships between their communities was even more obscure. Today, scientists understand that, while plant associations do vary according to elevation, those associations are not fixed in any way. Still, Merriam's system is a useful launching pad for understanding rudimentary ecological principles.

What is so extraordinary about the Grand Canyon is that, between the Grand Wash Cliffs on the west and the Marble Platform on the east, five of Merriam's seven zones are fully represented. An ascent from the Inner Gorge to the Kaibab Plateau is, in effect, the environmental equivalent of a two-thousand-mile change in geographical latitude. That is to say, a hike from the river bottom up Tapeats Creek to Monument Point is analogous, biologically speaking, to a hike from the state of Sonora in northern Mexico clear up past the Canadian border. Only quicker.

The actual altitude change within the region we have been discussing is 7,600 feet—from its lowest point at the foot of the Grand Wash Cliffs near Lake Mead (1,200 feet) to its highest at Point Imperial on the North Rim near Grand Canyon Lodge (8,801 feet). If we confine drab statistics to the core of the park itself, it is still a 5,790-foot descent from the North Kaibab Trailhead to the confluence of Bright Angel Creek and the river. Or, put another way for those who detest long walks, a short stroll along the South Rim from the El Tovar Hotel bar to the Powell Memorial, and a deftly executed swan dive off Hopi Point into Horn Creek Rapid, will afford one a free fall of just under a mile. Latitudinally speaking, this is a free fall from Calgary, Alberta, to Hermosillo, Mexico. Well, not so free, actually. There are a few ledges to whack along the way.

While the life zones in the Grand Canyon are rather loosely configured, they are useful in helping to identify the plant and animal communities one comes across on any wandering (or free fall) between river and rim. We have to bear in mind, of course, that Merriam's system is very oversimplified. There are variances in precipitation and moisture retention, as well as broad temperature fluctuations (the controlling factor in determining zones) between north- and south-facing slopes of the same elevation. Wind contributes a cooling

The vista from Powell Monument, named for the man who first explored the mysteries of the Grand Canyon. In 1869 virtually nothing was known of this labyrinthine canyon or the river that carved it. Major John Wesley Powell, with a company of ten men and four boats, set forth on May 24, 1869 to explore "the Great Unknown"—a journey that proved to be one of the great adventures in the history of American discovery.

influence on exposed plateaus and is less a determinant in sheltered areas. Soil composition and conditions vary, as do evaporation conditions, and all these considerations influence the presence of plant and animal communities.

Nevertheless, every zone has its "indicator" species of plants and animals, and if we know what zone we're in, we pretty much know what flora and fauna we're likely to encounter. Conversely, if we know what plant and animal we're looking at, we know, more or less, what zone we're in. To many visitors, this may seem of marginal interest, but consider the practical side. We know we're not going to have to shake the scorpions out of our shoes when we're camping in the boreal forests of the Kaibab Plateau, because the only species of scorpion that is potentially lethal, *Centruroides sculptuatus*, is an inhabitant of the Lower Sonoran; conversely, we know our postprandial nap on the beach below Deubendorff Rapid isn't going to be interrupted by the squawking of some psychotic Steller's jay or the chattering of disputatious red squirrels. Neither jays nor squirrels are encountered below the Transition zone. So there you have it. Amazing how a little knowledge always brings comfort.

In the Grand Canyon, the life zones begin with the Lower Sonoran of the Inner Gorge, which includes, of course, the riparian corridor of the river itself. The construction of Glen Canyon Dam in 1963 altered this habitat in major (many would argue catastrophic) ways, not the least of which was the lowering of the water temperature to between forty-two and forty-five degrees, and the reduction of the sediment load from an estimated 380,000 tons per day to 40,000 tons per day. For native fish accustomed to temperatures that fluctuated from near freezing during the winter to seventy-five degrees during the summer, the change was disastrous. Spawning and the hatching of eggs became difficult at best, and for some species impossible. So the roundtail chub and the Colorado squawfish are now extinct in the Grand Canyon. The razorbacked sucker is virtually extinct. Bonytail and humpback chubs are endangered, their spawning grounds having been reduced to the Little Colorado and possibly some of the creeks farther downstream.

The good news, depending on one's proclivities, is the introduction of a thriving population of rainbow and brown trout—prosperous fish in a cold river rich in nutrients like phosphorous that get imported from Lake Powell through the penstocks of the dam. Phosphorous feeds an alga called *Cladophora glomerata*, which feeds a one-celled organism called a diatom, which feeds a crustacean called an amphipod, which feeds a trout, which feeds a happy angler—or possibly one of the hundred or so bald eagles who have taken up winter residence in the canyon as a consequence of this post-dam cornucopia.

It would be gratifying to announce that along the Colorado River and its tributary streams the dominant "indicator" plants are still the seep willow, coyote willow, desert broom, and the Fremont cottonwood, but sadly this is a highly debatable issue. The dominant plant is a noxious foreign weed called tamarisk (actually a bony tree impersonating an anorexic

Bunch grass grows among the rocks on the North Rim above Dead Horse Mesa.

FOLLOWING PAGES:

The Colorado cuts a horse-shoe bend around Point Hansbrough. In time the river may eat its way through the base of this great meander and carve the point away from the plateau.

TRAILS OF THE WILD BURRO

The Spanish first brought the African burro to North America, where the animal's ability to withstand long periods without water made it the preferred beast of burden for southwestern prospectors. Many of the animals escaped or were abandoned by their hard-scrabble owners. Since female burros can reproduce about every eighteen months, they proliferated at an astronomical rate. Unfortunately burros are prodigious and indiscriminate eaters, stripping the desert of its vegetation, competing with native species like mule deer and bighorn sheep, and pounding the earth into networks of erosion-causing trails. At one time feral burros were an enormous problem in the Grand Canyon, and until 1980 the Park Service controlled them by shooting them on sight. Since 1981 a more humane program to round them up and relocate them has effectively eliminated their presence.

shrub) that was imported from Asia into the Southwest in the mid-1800s as a form of erosion control. It has metastasized up every river in the American West, choking out native vegetation, destroying the indigenous habitat, taking over beaches, and consuming vast quantities of water with its interminable root system. One must not be deceived by what some of the guidebooks refer to as the "feathery grace" or the "delicate perfume" of the tamarisk. It is a biological nightmare, an abomination, the Bela Lugosi of herbal life.

Fortunately, coyote willow seems to be making a comeback, and anyway, tamarisk confines itself to the banks of drainage systems and hasn't yet crowded out indigenous species just back from the river. One still encounters varieties of "characteristic" vegetation in the Lower Sonoran—like mesquite, catclaw acacia, creosote bush, four-winged saltbush, and barrel and beavertail cactus.

Of these natives we are obliged to pay our highest tribute to the creosote bush, a truly sociopathic plant that exudes a toxin into the ground around itself to ward off competition for the infrequent rains that sustain it. Given the chance, it will even poison its own offspring. Small wonder that specimens of the creosote shrub have been determined to be the oldest living things on earth, even older than the bristlecone pine.

Hikers and rafters along the riparian banks of the Lower Sonoran zone are likely to encounter a number of associated animals—often at dawn or dusk, but particularly at night, since most of them are nocturnal. Beavers, which in the Grand Canyon have a light, orangish-brown coloring, are more likely to be heard than seen. Being waked in the middle of the night to what sounds like somebody smacking the water with a paddle is something most river runners have experienced at one time or another. A far more common sighting is the ringtail, an animal that looks a bit like a guilty cat with a raccoon's tail (it is, in fact, a member of the raccoon family). It has become so accustomed to humans that you can often see it sliding around the fringes of your campsite, or slipping onto a beached raft to inspect the quality of the provisions. Its first cousin, the common raccoon, is uncommon in the canyon, but spotted skunks are plentiful enough and are equipped with the same defense mechanism as the larger, striped skunk. More elusive than ringtails, they are sometimes encountered during that bladder-inspired 3:00 A.M. stumble from sleeping bag to beach, and one can pay dearly for an interview. It's hard to get back to sleep after one has been anointed.

And, of course, we must not forget everybody's favorite Lower Sonoran creature-feature, the humble scorpion. In the Grand Canyon there are six species of this arachnid, but only the skinny, little, straw-colored variety known as the "slender scorpion" can seriously ruin one's day. Like most creatures in the canyon, they are nocturnal, and they are prone to scuttle under a tarp, or into a shoe, at the first sign of daylight. Recognition is not always easy, but their consistent yellow color, narrow pincers, and the oblong segments of their very svelte tail (an eighth inch, maximum) are a help. If, when you find one skulking in your socks, you remain in doubt, you can always poke it with your pinky. And if, after it has stung you, your finger gets numb, and your arm begins to tingle as though you'd slept on it, and you begin to drool, and have trouble talking and breathing, and go into convulsions, and lose your sense of sight—well, congratulations, you've made a positive identification.

The chances of confusing the Grand Canyon rattlesnake with any other species found in the inner canyon—the striped whip snake, common king snake, western garter snake—are slim. These three reptiles are all members of the racer family and have the slender head typical of their group. The Grand Canyon rattlesnake, however—a subspecies of the western rattlesnake—has the triangular head of the pit viper, comes in a distinctive dusty pink color, and is the only thing in the Lower Sonoran zone with rattles on its tail. Moreover, it dislikes humanity and keeps its distance, so the chance of seeing it at all is remote.

Humans are the least of a rattler's problems. It is the blue plate special for hawks, eagles, ringtails, skunks, coyotes, and various other snakes, particularly king snakes. It is highly susceptible to intense heat, from which it can die in a matter of minutes, and to cold, which can immobilize it in an unprotected place and turn it into a predator's lunch. It is sometimes the victim of its own appetite, dying in the process of trying to swallow something so big that it is rendered virtually helpless.

Better to be reincarnated as a harvester ant. We can't leave the Lower Sonoran without a word about this little pestilence. Desert campers and river runners call these cheery little pests fire ants, and not because of their color. A seed-stashing Formicida that lays up great supplies of food in caches ten feet and deeper in the ground—and that has survived the hottest and most arid conditions for millions upon millions of years—it establishes itself in massive colonies generated by a single queen, who mates but once and goes on producing eggs for up to two decades. It is apparently the responsibility of her multitudinous offspring to hang around campsites frequented by the crumb-dropping Homo sapiens, waiting for an opportunity to crawl between a flip-flop and a big toe and register a presence.

The sting of a harvester ant is an elevating experience, one that is way out of proportion to the size of its perpetrator, one that can leave its recipient massively indifferent to everything but the eradication of ANTS in general, family, genus, and species—not to mention the single, felonious individual. The bite of a fire ant almost always results in the flinging of the flip-flops into the river and the reintroduction of shoes and socks. In truth, the only thing positive to be said about these pandemic little buggers is that they are diurnal and go to bed early.

Above the Inner Gorge, the Upper Sonoran (3,500 to 7,000 feet) extends from the Tonto Platform to a point somewhere between the talus slopes of Hermit shale and the sheer cliffs of the Coconino sandstone. This zone has no clear lines of demarcation. Elevation, temperature, exposure, and soil composition all play important parts in determining the fuzzy boundaries of these belts, and precipitation is unquestionably among the most critical ingredients. The Upper Sonoran may get a smidgen more rainfall than the Lower (eight to ten inches annually as opposed to four to six), but it's clear from a quick look around that a smidgen is a mite less than enough—at least for anything luxurious to prosper.

On the Kaibab Plateau, most of the desert vegetation found in the canyon gives way to ponderosa pine forest, aspen groves, and, in sunny spots, Rocky Mountain maples.

Seeps and springs are found most often on the north side of the canyon, where they nourish patches of water-loving plants. These oases result when water percolates through the Kaibab limestone of the rim and runs through cracks and fissures in the underlying layers of rock, eventually flowing outward to the canyon wall.

Most inner canyon plants have adapted to conditions of heat and drought by developing small, waxy, or leathery leaves that reduce the amount of moisture lost to evaporation.

BIOTIC COMMUNITIES
OF THE GRAND CANYON

Animal and botanical life in the Grand Canyon extends from desert-dwelling Sonoran and Mojave species to boreal and subalpine communities commonly found in mountain forests. Plants range from the maidenhair fern, which requires constant moisture, to the Utah agave, which requires very little. Animals run the gamut from the mountain lion and the bobcat to the collard lizard and the whipsnake. The canyon is home to one of the rarest and most beautiful squirrels (the Kaibab) in the United States, one of its ugliest lizards (the chuckwalla), its noblest bird (the bald eagle), and its most promiscuous ant (the harvester).

Given the fact that there is an elevation difference of approximately six thousand feet between the river and the rim, this diversity is not surprising. Temperature, moisture, elevation, and exposure to sunlight are the major

The Kaibab squirrel is a hostage to his own dietary restrictions. Feeding only on the bark and seeds of the ponderosa pine, he is trapped on the Kaibab Plateau—an island of forest surrounded on three sides by desert and on the fourth by a mile-deep canyon.

Patches of big sage (below) inter-
mingle with stands of ponderosa
pine on both rims of the canyon.

Canyon nights are heralded by the song
of the coyote. This extremely adaptable
animal feeds on a variety of canyon
residents, including mice, squirrels,
rabbits, reptiles, birds, and insects. It
makes its den alongside river banks
and in canyon walls.

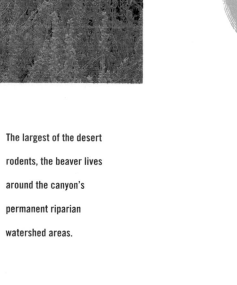

The largest of the desert
rodents, the beaver lives
around the canyon's
permanent riparian
watershed areas.

INVASION OF THE TAMARISK

Tamarisk, or salt-cedar, is a non-native species that was introduced into the United States during the early part of the twentieth century. A number of varieties were imported by the Department of Agriculture as an erosion control device, and over the last seventy-five years they have spread up virtually every major watercourse in the American West. Writer Ann Zwinger has said of them: "They are weedy, grasping trees that form ugly thickets and are fire hazards . . . their greedy roots and the dense shade of their thickets make it impossible for native plants to get started." Tamarisks have long, web-like roots that can travel twenty or thirty feet across a beach to reach water, and they generally grow eight to ten feet tall. Their thin, scaly stems have feathery branches, and they blossom in showy pink plumes.

The dominant plant of the lower reaches of this zone is blackbrush, and blackbrush is a very sorry looking piece of work—low-growing, tangled, spiky branched, with small, leathery leaves. Even when a wet spring induces it to flower, it can only muster a dreary bouquet of tiny, yellowish blooms that look more dead than alive. Of course, to liven things up, there's Mormon tea, a broomlike shrub with tiny yellow flowers that can be brewed into a dubious drink, and many varieties of cacti—the beavertail, prickly pear, and Whipple cholla being the most easily identifiable.

The Upper Sonoran also sports forests of banana yucca (a member of the lily family) and Utah agave (a member of the amaryllis family, also known as the "century plant"). The two look vaguely similar and are sometimes confused, but the agave is easily distinguished by its sawtoothed leaves. The flowering habits of the two plants are also very different. The agave sits around sulking for twenty to twenty-five years without putting out so much as a blossom, and then, in a matter of a few days, shoots up one skinny stalk about fifteen feet high and dies. The yucca, on the other hand, puts up creamy blooms annually in the spring and apparently feels no need for morbid histrionics. The Anasazi, ancestors of the modern Hopi, who inhabited these canyons from about 500 to 1300 A.D., fermented the agave roots to make an alcoholic drink and used the roots of the yucca as a laxative. One must surmise they had no difficulty distinguishing between the two plants.

At the upper margins of this zone, we find what are perhaps the most characteristic (and certainly most aromatic) of southwestern desert plants—the big sagebrush (*Artemisia tridentata*, a member of the sunflower family) and the juniper/pinyon woodland, home to the extremely raucous pinyon jay, the only slightly less noisy rock squirrel, and the tiny pinyon mouse. This rodent, with its inch-long ears, scorns the tree from which it derives its name and does its feeding and nesting in juniper trees.

Antelope ground squirrels are also common (no relation to the jackalope). They live in cool burrows, but are often seen during the day, scampering back and forth with their cheeks stuffed with seeds and their tails fanned out over their backs to protect themselves from the sun. What these rodents have in common with antelope is a mystery.

What will not any longer be found in this climatic zone (or in any other zone in the Grand Canyon, for that matter) is the cute little African burro. *Equus asinus*, with its fuzzy ears and perky eye, is the faunal equivalent of the plague, and it is encouraging to report its absence. Once the faithful companion of nineteenth-century prospectors, the diminutive ass became the Grand Canyon's version of the Terminator, demolishing vegetation by completely stripping vast areas and pounding them to dust, cutting fantastic infrastructures of erosion-inducing trails, competing with mule deer and desert bighorn sheep for territory, and trampling archaeological sites. Burros made the side-hill cowgit look like a harmless browser.

For years, it was Park Service policy to shoot these pests on sight, but howls of protest by animal rights advocates and lovers of all things furry led to an expensive, though apparently successful, program to save the environment by "relocating" the burro—i.e., zapping the beasts with a sedative gun and hauling them off to other climes.

Both the North and South Rims of the Grand Canyon lie within the Transition zone (7,000 feet to 8,250 feet), and it is here, where annual rainfall varies from fifteen to twenty-two inches and average midsummer temperatures remain in the high seventies and low eighties, that the ponderosa pine forest dominates the scene. Around Grand Canyon Village on the South Rim, ponderosa mixes primarily with juniper/pinyon woodland; on the North Rim, with manzanita, mountain mahogany, Gambel oak, and aspen.

Although C. Hart Merriam divided the terrain above the canyon rims into two separate zones, for our purposes they are better described simply as "Kaibab Plateau," a domain of conifers, aspens, grassy meadows, and the smell of pine resin. Along the North Rim and moving up from it to an elevation of about 8,200 feet (on the South Rim the slope is downward to about 6,500 feet) the ponderosa forest is open, and the understory unobstructed. One finds scattered stands of Gambel oak and mountain mahogany, occasional patches of sagebrush or thorny locust, and some pinyon and juniper at the lower levels. But the overall impression is of tall, well-spaced trees above a soft carpet of pine duff. Nothing here to stick, prick, scratch, or bite—at least not much.

At its highest elevations (8,200 to 9,200 feet) this airy terrain graduates into more dense and tangled vegetation. The ponderosa gives way to dark woods of white fir, Douglas fir, and Engelmann spruce, interrupted now and then by groves of aspen. This is the domain of horned owls and horned toads, mountain chickadees and mountain blue birds, hermit thrushes, ruby-crowned kinglets, and solitary vireos, porcupines, chipmunks, various flavors of mouse, and the obnoxious, disorderly, raucous, endlessly jabbering annoyance known as the red squirrel. It is just as chittering and ill-tempered in the Kaibab boreal forest as it is in the woods of northern Vermont.

But it is lower down in the ponderosa plantation that the more interesting rodent story unfolds. About a million years ago, the Abert and Kaibab squirrels were one and the same species—or at the very least, closely related. They are the same size, their "bark" is the same, both have reddish backs, bluish-gray flanks, and ear tassels; both are "tied" to the ponderosa pine as the exclusive source of their diet. They eat its blossoms in the spring, seeds from the cones (as well as a fungus that grows beneath the tree) during the summer, and the inner bark of twigs during the winter. And that's pretty much it. Without ponderosa, neither the Abert nor the Kaibab squirrel can survive.

The only difference between the two animals is that the Abert squirrel has a white breast, belly, and underside of the tail; the Kaibab has a dark gray belly and a great, snow-white plume of a tail that makes it one of the most magnificent specimens of its biological family. Why the two have evolved in this separate fashion is something of a mystery, since there seems to be no obvious adaptive purpose served by the differentiation.

*L*ooking south from Point Imperial, the canyon is awash in early morning light. Because of the high elevation of this part of the Kaibab Plateau, ponderosa pine grows far down into the canyon.

A thick duff of pine
needles provides a soft
carpet for hikers along
the North Rim.

Winter shuts down the North Rim. The roads are blocked by snow; campgrounds and visitor facilities are closed. Except for the occasional cross country skier, the wild inhabitants are left undisturbed by humans from October to May.

How these evolutionary differences came about is another matter. As the low-lands in northern Arizona were slowly transformed into deserts between two million and ten thousand years ago, the ponderosa pine was forced to higher and higher elevations. Forests that once extended completely across the canyon receded upward, and the squirrels on the North Rim were eventually isolated, their range reduced to the 350-square-mile area of the Kaibab Plateau where ponderosa still thrives. Except for several locations around Mount Logan and Mount Trumbull, where the animal has been translocated by the Arizona Department of Game and Fish, it is, in fact, the only place in the world where the Kaibab squirrel is found—since to go courting on the South Rim (or anywhere else), the northern swains would have had to cross either the canyon or the desert, and without their seeds and twigs and truffles they wouldn't do it.

These elegant but unadaptable rodents are joined in their transition environment by a number of animals, none of which is so confined by dietary choice and, hence, by a single vegetational zone. There are mountain lions, those "deadly enemies of the deer" (to quote Teddy Roosevelt, who delighted in hunting them). Along with wolves, coyotes, bobcats, and great horned owls, mountain lions were killed by the hundreds during the early part of this century in an ill-conceived attempt to protect the Kaibab's mule deer and blue grouse. The lions have apparently made a gradual comeback, and current estimates are that about sixty pair now inhabit the broken rocks and side canyons near the rim.

The bobcats and coyotes are also thriving—particularly the coyotes, who rival the cockroach for most likely to inherit the earth. And the mule deer population, which has boomed and busted at least twice since human beings started tinkering with an ecological balance they scarcely understood, seems equally healthy.

The Kaibab deer story is everybody's favorite Ecology Lesson #1. That's the "don't mess with the natural order of things or Mother Nature will spank" lesson. In 1906, when Theodore Roosevelt established the Grand Canyon Game Preserve, the size of the Kaibab deer herd was estimated to be around four thousand animals. To improve on these figures, government hunters were sent out to eliminate predators, which they did with a vengeance, and in less than twenty years the deer population soared to one hundred thousand. Enter the drought of 1924. The badly overtaxed habitat simply could no longer support such a massive community, and over the next five years, 90 percent of the mule deer on the Kaibab starved and died. Unfortunately, Mother Nature spanked the wrong party. She should have taken Mr. Roosevelt and his janissaries to the woodshed, not the deer.

On the other hand, the Kaibab deer revived, overpopulated, and crashed once again in 1954, this time without the help of government hunters or natural predators. So one is left to conclude that either human tinkering screwed things up so badly in the first place that matters can never be naturally restored or we don't really understand much about the long-term stability of animal populations. It's a relatively new science, ecology; it's been only 128 years

The scarcity of natural predators in the park means that visitors to the North Rim photograph more mule deer than any other animal. In the winter, the deer normally descend to lower elevations. During the spring and summer months, however, they are often found grazing in the grassy basins and open meadows of the plateau.

Elves Chasm, with its clear pools and fern gardens, is a favorite spot for Colorado River runners.

In the midst of the towering grandeur—spires, buttes, cliffs, walls, and great stone ledges—it's easy to miss the canyon's humbler beauties, such as white flowering verbena at Fossil Canyon Beach.

The rocks of the Inner Gorge are the oldest exposed rocks in the Grand Canyon. Radiometrically dated between 1.7 and 2 billion years, they have been called the basement of the North American continent.

since the German Darwinian, Ernst Haeckel, even came up with the term. Given the time scale we're working with here at the Grand Canyon, that's about a nanosecond.

And, of course, once we get back to pondering environmental issues in terms of geological time, the importance of human intervention in nature's ecosystem management takes on a rather different perspective. It is undoubtedly true that in the Kaibab Plateau region man is largely, if not entirely, responsible for the demise of a number of species—the wolf, the bear, the jaguar, the condor, the burrowing owl, the Colorado squawfish, the roundtail chub, and a good many others. And it is equally true that he is guilty of massively altering the composition of the vegetation along the riparian corridor of the Colorado River, of fouling the air over most of the canyon country, and of invading the peace and quiet of the entire region. In terms of millennia, how much will it matter?

Which is no apology or justification for insensibility. Being a Good Neighbor Sam in nature's community is still the right thing to do . . . but because it's right, not because it's going to make much difference in the very long run. Just stand out there at Lipan Point and wait a few million years. Another landscape Day of Judgment will surely arrive.

In the early 1980s I came to a decision that so vastly improved my quality of life I only regret that I didn't think of it twenty years sooner. Struggling up the Thunder River Trail, from the mouth of Tapeats Creek to Monument Point, with the temperature about 104 and the sole of my left boot starting to disengage from its vamp and quarter, I realized how bitterly I loathed walking—particularly up a 40 percent grade with a pack on my back. "This is it," I told the raven peering down at me from a ledge across the ravine. "Nevermore."

Stories of seventy-five-year-old grandmothers cruising the Bright Angel Trail notwithstanding, I have stuck to my guns. Day hikes only. Short ones. Carry nothing but smoked trout, Carr's water crackers, havarti, Spanish olives, a bottle of Leflaive Montrachet '77, and a truffle. Forget lugging all those plastic bottles of water around. Nobody ever died with an unfinished Montrachet in their pack. Leave late, return early, schedule time for a recuperative nap.

So it happens that in mid-October of 1994 my wife, Lynn, and I are on our way from Lees Ferry to Pipe Springs when we decide to detour (she demands we detour) to the North Rim for a trot out to Widforss Point— which is on my short list of acceptable trots, and which many people regard as the most enchanting of North Rim walks. It is short and easy (ten

On the North Rim between seven to eight thousand feet, ponderosa pines are found growing in relatively pure stands. Aspens, which at higher elevations tend to comingle with spruce and fir, are more commonly found along the edge of meadows and in open spaces in the forest.

THE EDGE OF THE FOREST

miles round-trip), relatively level, restricted to foot travel—and, as it crosses the entire range of Kaibab forest environments on its way to an overlook into the great maw of the Awful Gorge, it offers the best of both rim and plateau. The fact that it snowed eight inches last night only whets Lynn's appetite.

Three miles short of Grand Canyon Lodge, a dirt road leaves the paved highway from Jacob Lake, curves around a wooded slope, and crosses a grassy meadow to the Widforss Trailhead marker. We walk the road because it is closed by snow, and I protest that it looks like it might snow again, maybe we ought to reconsider, but I do not prevail and am marched smartly forward under the stinging lash of my partner's contempt.

The path rises from the end of the meadow and traverses a gentle (I argue steep) slope of ponderosa, spruce, and aspen, before leveling off along the upper reaches of Transept Canyon. The Transept is actually a side canyon feeding into Bright Angel Canyon—which, in turn, feeds into the main canyon of the Colorado—but like all these overgrown ravines, it is huge, deep, and utterly inhospitable. Much better viewed, I suggest, from its eastern side, through the windows of the cozy dining room at Grand Canyon Lodge. Over tea and cookies.

For about three miles, the path follows the western contour of the Transept, periodically poking out to the edge for fantastic views to the south. From a spur where my whining finally procures a rest stop, we can see across eleven miles of tributary canyons, amphitheaters, buttes, mesas, ledges, and alcoves to the near vertical wall of the South Rim, somewhere around Moran Point. In the foreground lies the abyss, in the middle ground the creamy, Coconino caprock of Deva, Brahma, and Zoroaster Temples. Against the distant horizon, seventy miles beyond Angels Gate, Wotans Throne, and Vishnu Temple, the lofty volcanic peaks of the San Francisco Mountains mark the southern boundary of the Colorado Plateau. Very white on top, I glumly observe.

At some points along the North Rim, the mixed ponderosa, white, and Douglas fir forest extends well over the brink and down into the canyon for about four or five hundred feet—whereupon it gives way to scattered stands of pinyon, juniper, mountain mahogany, blackbrush, and sage. Along the Widforss Trail, the typical plateau species stop at the rim and change rather abruptly, as one descends, to cliffrose, Gambel oak, pinyon, juniper.

We switchback around several ravines that feed into the Transept and then angle away from the rim. Through the woods the slender, bleached trunks of aspen are interspersed among the conifers, and their leaves, fluttering down from stark and bony branches, lay scattered on the snow like golden inlays in a slab of pure Makrana marble. The air is getting dry and brittle with the cold.

Coming up out of a shallow valley through venerable ponderosa over a hundred feet tall and probably twice as old, many of which have been scarred by lightning

Much of the snow and rainwater on the Kaibab Plateau collects in limestone basins and sinks such as Little Park Lake on the North Rim. The water eventually percolates through the layers of rock beneath and reemerges at seeps and springs thousands of feet below on the canyon walls.

strikes, we scare up a herd of turkeys, the first sign of wildlife we've seen—other than squirrel tracks and an inordinately healthy-looking coyote trotting along the edge of the meadow at the trailhead.

We might have had better luck if we were making this trek back in 1905, and the federal government hadn't yet established the Grand Canyon National Game Preserve, much of it on the Kaibab Plateau. The only game "preserved" was the ubiquitous and still fawned-over mule deer, who, not being eaten by lions, wolves, and coyotes, overpopulated and ate themselves (so to speak) out of house and home. Between 1906 and 1930, something like five thousand coyotes, one thousand mountain lions, and five hundred bobcat were shot by game wardens and helpful "sportsmen," though these statistics are a little suspect and vary from account to account.

Although the wolves are gone, the mountain lion and bobcat have returned in relatively small numbers. But our chances of encountering any representatives of the cat family are slim to none. Coyote, fox, deer, and wild turkeys, maybe, and perhaps the Kaibab squirrel, who stores up no food for winter and does not head for a burrow when the snow flies like more sensible red squirrels, chipmunks, wood rats, harvest mice, and middle-aged gentlemen unencumbered by athletic wives.

If this were summer, we would be enjoying a variety of plants and flowers that are now buried under the snow or have tucked back until their season comes again. There would be wild strawberries, astors, peavine, and specklepod locoweed, dwarf hollygrape, and scarlet-colored skyrockets. But we are passing into the quiet zone; the brown stalks of bracken poke above the frozen mantle, and the flutelike song of the hermit thrush will not be heard until summer.

For about a mile and a half, the trail goes up a long ravine and through a mature stand of russet-barked ponderosa before it terminates at Widforss Point. We stop to listen to the hammering of a hairy woodpecker (or could that be my heart?) and comment that he seems to be a little behind the eight ball in getting his acorns laid up. The trees are tall, widely spaced, and virtually without understory, and we can tell just from the change in the quality of light that we are almost on the rim.

And then suddenly the forest ends. There is a narrow band of sloping, desert vegetation—juniper, pinyon, Gambel oak, cliffrose, Apache plume, and hedgehog cactus—a picnic spot and tiny camping area, and a rocky spine leading to a small overlook. The huffing hiker either quits here and unpacks his lunch, or executes a three-thousand-foot head plant into Haunted Canyon. The actual Widforss Point lies a few thousand feet to the left, between an unnamed drainage on the east and the upper reaches of Haunted Canyon on the west. But however you define the trail's end, it's a precipitous drop of over three thousand feet to the bottom.

Also known as the desert Spanish bayonet, rare Whipple's yucca is occasionally found along the Colorado River between the Grand Wash Cliffs and Kanab Creek. It is related to the commonly found banana yucca. Both plants are members of the lily family.

A view across Buddha Temple to the South Rim of the Grand Canyon. The Transept Canyon drainage below joins Bright Angel Creek just above Phantom Ranch.

caly combinations of fungus and algae—the main components of lichen—create intricate patterns of color.

As I predicted, at about the time I am uncorking the Montrachet and delaminating the plastic wrap from the smoked trout, it begins to snow again, lightly. Lynn could care less, so enraptured is she of the vista—the great western wall of Manu Temple immediately in front of us, Buddha Temple beyond, and the endless cacophony of buttes, buttresses, points, pyramids, terraces, and cathedrals soaring out of the "awesome cavity" that defies narration.

I could do better describing the wine and fish than the view. Clarence Dutton, the first geologist to study the plateau, observed, "It is perhaps in some respects unfortunate that the stupendous pathway of the Colorado River through the Kaibabs was ever called a cañon, for the name identifies it with the baser conception." The simple noun gives no concept of proportion, ornamentation, design, color, and atmosphere. "All of these attributes combine with infinite complexity to produce a whole which at first bewilders and at length overpowers."

A sentiment to which I fully subscribe. The Montrachet, on the other hand, is almost as complex as the Grand Canyon—without surpassing comprehension.

SACRED DATURA

The datura plant (Datura metaloides), *also known as sacred datura, is a member of the potato family and is common in the Grand Canyon. It grows twenty to seventy inches high, with large, trumpet-shaped, white flowers that bloom at night and look like overgrown petunias. During the day the blossoms turn purplish or brown. Sacred datura contains several alkaloids, including atropine and hyoscyamine, and is highly poisonous. Datura seed pods are commonly found in southwestern archaeological sites, where Indian cultures used the plant for both ceremonial and medicinal purposes. In the appropriate amount it is an effective anesthetic; it also produces powerful hallucinations. The critical issue is "appropriate amount." Every now and then some misinformed drug culture miscreant tries eating sacred datura, and departs from the canyon in a body bag.*

Quaking or trembling aspen acquired its name from the constant rustling of its foliage, which flutters in the slightest breeze.

September 18: It is early fall. High up on the Kaibab Plateau, a few stands of aspen have jumped the gun and are starting to show tints of yellow. An autumn breeze blows through the spruce and fir, and the red squirrels are going frantically about their last-minute winter storage. But down here on the Marble Platform, the air temperature is still in the upper eighties, the rocks along the Colorado riverbank are hot enough to fry a rasher of bacon, and the water is its customary forty-eight degrees. Standing in it for more than twenty seconds makes the legs burn with the cold.

There are fourteen of us at Lees Ferry, blowing up the boats, tying down raft frames and oars, loading on waterproof duffel bags, rocket cans, ammo cans, dry boxes, water containers, fire pans, medical kits, repair kits, pumps, spare life jackets, and twenty-four cases of beer for barter and trade. Commercial operators hog the ramp with their thirty-foot baloney boats and mountains of gear, but we will endure their snarling outboard engines for only a few days as they pass us going down the river. Then their season is over. Only oar-powered rafts are permitted after September 24.

It is nearly dark by the time we are rigged, and we head for the trucks, drive up the narrow access road that leads down from Highway 89 to the confluence of the

INTO THE MADCAP UNKNOWN

Colorado and Paria Rivers. We take our places in the dining room of the Marble Canyon Lodge at the foot of the Vermillion Cliffs. Order up the Last Supper. Great merriment amongst my compadres, and a plethora of bad boatmen jokes, but I feel like Major Powell when he wrote, "We are now ready to start on our way down the Great Unknown." His companions remained cheerful, he said. "Jests are bandied about freely this morning; but to me the cheer is somber and the jests are ghastly."

It has taken my wife, Lynn, nine years of annually renewing herself on a Park Service waiting list to secure a private permit to run the Colorado through the Grand Canyon, and in that time I have gone from a lean, mean, forty-seven-year-old light-heavyweight to an oleaginous, fifty-six-year-old cruiser-weight with bad nerves. Although I've only had one serious wreck in fifteen years of river running (flipping on the Dolores River in a poisonous and mean-spirited rapid called Snaggletooth), the Colorado has many Snaggleteeth on its menu, plus a few dozen rotten molars, and my bad dreams on the tarmac at Lees Ferry are of maelstroms like Unkar, Hance, Sockdolager, Grapevine, Horn, Hermit, Granite, Crystal, Deubendorff, Lava. Martin Litton, the founder of Grand Canyon Dories, used to comfort anxious passengers who asked about the severity of any given rapid by rolling his eyes and intoning, "Horrible. Just terrifying."

Yes, well, Martin has been down this river so many times he can afford to be whimsical. For the rest of us, the Colorado's rapids are ranked on a scale of difficulty from one to ten, and there are, by my count (and depending on the water level), about twenty-five that are ranked six or above, fourteen rated seven or above, nine judged to be eight or above, and then there's Crystal and Lava falls. For some reason, Crystal is the one that has truly captured my imagination—no doubt because, after its rearrangement by the 1983 flood, it has become the most dangerous in which to make an error. On the other hand, any rapid is dangerous when you make the right error. Horrible. Terrifying.

The National Park Service assigns about 90 percent of the user days on the river to commercial operators, a policy that may have seemed reasonable when few people possessed the skill or equipment to run the canyon. But today it can only be regarded as an overallocation of a public resource to private enterprise. So I hold the river ranger's office responsible for my declining eagerness to row Class 10 rapids. I just got too old and fat while I waited. And from the look of things going into the huge coolers we carry with us, I'm not going to get any skinnier on this trip. The problem is how to get it all onto four eighteen-foot rafts and still have room for passengers.

Which happens to present us with our first interpersonal friction. We have amongst us a young boatman whose culinary taste leans toward seeds and nuts, and whose opinion of our floating restaurant and bar is perhaps less than generous. He isn't happy with his boat either, an old Havasu with warped oars, but he is pretty much ignored. Other differences will arise as we descend "the Great Unknown," but for the moment we are still one big blissful family.

A small waterfall cuts through the granite bed of Pipe Creek.

John Wesley Powell gave Marble Canyon its misleading name because the water-polished limestone exposed at river level has the smoothness and sheen of fine marble.

September 20: Our camp tonight is at mile thirty-four, just below Redwall Cavern. We have thus far survived a civil disorder at Navajo Bridge, numerous Class 5 river uprisings at Badger Creek, Soap Creek, House Rock, North Canyon, and 24-1/2 and 25 Mile Rapids, and a weight watcher's dinner on our first night featuring turkey with stuffing, mashed potatoes, cranberry sauce, broccoli, tossed salad, and chocolate pie.

The bridge incident (a couple of kids depth-bomb us with small chunks of sandstone as we float 470 feet underneath them), reminded me of standing on that same span nearly fifty years ago with my parents and a bunch of people gathered at Marble Canyon for a Navajo rodeo. It was after dark, and my father (among others) was entertaining himself by dumping boxes of Diamond matches over the edge while Art Greene, owner of the lodge, filled a truck tire with gasoline. The matches fell head first and after an interminable wait, ignited in a showery sparkle on the rocks below. The truck tire, when lit and hurled over the railing, descended into the blackened void like a fiery comet in space, landed in the river with a terrific WHOMP, and floated along like Cleopatra's funeral barge until it disappeared around the bend at Six Mile Wash.

The river has provoked no inordinate challenge thus far. Below Soap Creek, we noted the obituary carved in the sandstone to Frank M. Brown, President of the Denver, Colorado Canon and Pacific Railroad Company. In 1889, Brown thought he could build a railroad through the Grand Canyon to haul coal from Colorado to San Diego, and he was equally certain that life jackets were a pointless nuisance on a surveying trip. Turned out to be wrong on both counts and drowned at about mile twelve, after he capsized in Soap Creek Rapid.

We doffed our hats at 24-1/2 Mile Rapid to Bert Loper, known as "the Grand Old Man of the Colorado," who drowned after he capsized here in 1949 at the age of almost eighty. And once again at 25 Mile Rapid to Peter Hansbrough and an unnamed companion, who were part of Brown's railroad survey party. Both drowned in 1889, a few days after Hansbrough carved the inscription to his boss below Soap Creek. Horrifying. Terrible.

I cannot say much for my own runs through either of the above riffles, except that I am alive, in camp, and bellied up to the trough when the pork chops, yams, broccoli, lingonberry sauce, cole slaw, and pineapple upside-down cake are being served. Our young boatman has shirked kitchen duty in favor of a photography hike (curious how the light is only suitable when there's work to be done), so we eat his portion and leave him the dishes. First law of the river, "you snooze, you lose," has broad application out here in the wilderness.

September 22: We are now ten miles below the confluence of the Colorado and Little Colorado, at the entrance to Unkar Rapid. The river is making its big westerly bend and is about to forsake Marble Canyon for the constricted walls of Granite Gorge. It will be nearly a hundred miles before things begin to open up again, but at least we know what we're in for—

The beach at Nankoweap on the lower right is a popular third-night camp for oar-powered river runners. High up on the cliff wall are Anasazi granaries, where the ancestors of the modern Hopi stored their corn and beans.

FOLLOWING PAGES:

Of Redwall Cavern, John Wesley Powell wrote in 1869: "The water sweeps rapidly in this elbow of river, and has cut its way under the rock, excavating a vast half circular chamber, which, if utilized for a theater, would give sitting to fifty thousand people."

These storage rooms for corn and beans have been abandoned since A.D. 1150 when, possibly because of prolonged drought, the Anasazi left the Grand Canyon region and moved southeast toward New Mexico.

more or less. I am reminded once again of Major Powell's over-quoted dirge—recorded, as a matter of fact, at this exact location: "We have an unknown distance yet to run; an unknown river yet to explore. What falls there are, we know not; what rocks beset the channel, we know not; what walls rise over the river, we know not. As well! we may conjecture many things."

The modern rafter's problem is that there are not enough things left to conjecture. Around every bend lies somebody's favorite side canyon, hike, historical site, archaeological site, or geological feature—and what with all the requisite stops at Vesey's Paradise, Redwall Cavern, Buck Farm Canyon, Nankoweap, and the Little Colorado (or the L.C., as it is affectionately known), we could well run out of rations before we get to Phantom Ranch. We killed two hours rolling around in the muck at the mouth of the L.C., and then the wind came up and started blowing us back up the river. Rowing a fully loaded, two-thousand-pound, flat-bottomed, rubber-tubed boat against a head wind is a great way to entertain yourself.

Neither George Bradley nor Jack Sumner of the Powell expedition thought much of the Little Colorado (né Flax, né Chiquito river)—"a loathsome little stream, so filthy and muddy that it fairly stinks" and "as disgusting a stream as there is on the continent; 3 rods wide and 3 ft. deep, half of its volume and 2/3 of its weight is mud and silt." But without the Little Colorado, the Colorado itself would need renaming. The sediment load that used to make the big river run red is now held back by Glen Canyon Dam, and it is only the "loathsome" little stream that reintroduces enough muck to give it back its proper color.

Bradley and Sumner thought the spring bursting out of the Redwall Cliff at Vesey's, with its great beard of mosses and ferns and flowering plants, one of the most beautiful sights they had ever seen. (And indeed it is a verdant, brilliant contrast to the monochromatic setting—red rocks/red river—that surrounds it.) Had they understood that it is fed by water sources that seep into the ground a mile up on the Kaibab Plateau, they might have also thought it one of the most amazing.

About the Anasazi ruins high above the river at Nankoweap Canyon, the Powell journals say nothing. Probably everybody was too busy with the rapid created by Nankoweap Creek to look up a thousand feet on the east-facing wall and see the little square doorways of these 800-year-old granaries. While carbon-14 testing of figurines found in a number of archaeological sites indicate that the Grand Canyon was inhabited as far back as four thousand years ago, the Pueblo period of the Anasazi culture (of which these granaries are a part) date from A.D. 750 to about A.D. 1100. By A.D. 1150—possibly as the consequence of a prolonged drought—Nankoweap, along with all other sites in the Grand Canyon, was abandoned. Now it is one of the premier photo stops for all river trips. And it always invokes the same question from the sweat-drenched, heart-pounding arrival who has just made the long, steep climb from the river to inspect it. "I wonder why they built it so damn far up?"

A glance at my handy waterproof edition of Buzz Belknap's *Grand Canyon River*

Guide (already soaked and its pages stuck together) tells me that tomorrow, in addition to the not-so-gentle swells at Unkar and Nevills Rapids, we have the dubious pleasure of rowing Hance, Sockdolager, Grapevine, Horn, and Granite. We are not talking here about dancing waters and modest waves. These are surging monsters with huge back waves, lateral waves, V-waves, tsunami waves, reversals, rocks, jagged, neoprene-ripping cliffs, whirlpools, boulder gardens, and boat-eating holes. The wretched hydraulics through these rapids can rip the oar from an oarsman's hands (usually with his arm still attached) as easily as King Kong tears up trees in the forest. These are Godzilla-meets-Bambi rapids. Dreadful. Horrible. Not suitable for elderly boatmen.

None of these thoughts are conducive to a good night's sleep, and as I lie in my sleeping bag staring up at what appear to be car lights on the rim near Desert View (the last point before exiting the eastern end of the park), I find the chile relleno casserole, chicken taco, tossed green salad, refries, and strawberry shortcake sitting a little heavy on the stomach. I think of the Anasazi and wonder if maybe they didn't have the right idea—abandon the canyon before it's too late. Who would know if I just snuck upstream to Tanner Canyon and high-tailed it up the trail that comes down from Lipan Point? My companions would just think I'd been wandering around in the dark and fell in the river. Swept away. Drowned. Alas, poor Yorick, and all that. Ah well! we may conjecture many things.

September 24: A short river day today, since yesterday was a long pull during which we stopped to scout five rapids and kill a few hours in the delicious, leafy shade of the cottonwoods at Phantom Ranch. Even in late September, the temperature on the river gets up into the nineties; anything green provides respite from the heat and glare on the water. The Kaibab and Bright Angel Trails converge here, and in the warm afternoon air, there is the heady aroma of road apples from the many mule trains that pass through.

Coming up from the beach to the Park Service buildings at the outwash of Bright Angel Canyon, there was a notice tacked on a post asking river runners to be on the lookout for the body of a drowned teenager somewhere between the Kaibab suspension bridge and Hermit Creek. The young man decided to swim across the river, apparently oblivious to the power of the current and the rapid loss of motor function in forty-five-degree water. He was, moreover, of the Frank M. Brown persuasion when it came to flotation devices, and tried it without a life jacket. A sad and costly error.

The posted notice was not good news—not for me, and not for the patient reader who is wondering why this narrative is fixated (apart from gluttony) on death and dying. The reason is because in the Grand Canyon the forces of nature are so obviously indifferent to all forms of two-legged life, craven cowards and stud muffins alike, that one's fragility and vulnerability is impossible to ignore. It is made manifest hour by hour, mile by mile, paragraph by paragraph.

Bighorn sheep are commonly seen along the banks of the river —unlike feral burros, who were removed from the park in 1981 because of their destructive impact on the environment.

Take last night. To the distant roll of thunder, we camped somewhere in the vicinity of 94 Mile Creek and ate a supper of curried chicken with condiments of raisins, sliced apples, Spanish peanuts, shredded coconut, chutney. We did dishes to a symphony of celestial booms and cracks somewhere up on the Kaibab Plateau; we laid out tarps and tents under the flash of strobe lightning and a bombardment of deafening explosions directly over our heads, amplified to ear-splitting volume by the sheer canyon walls.

Lynn and I huddled inside our Moss tent, a delicate little shelter of rip-stop nylon about as airy and insubstantial as Lady Astor's panties. We could hear waterfalls beginning to pour over the ledges a thousand feet above, gigantic cascades of soupy liquid, God's own mud slurry, gushing from the Tonto Platform and the North Rim, flowing down over the margins, washing another billion cubic yards of the Colorado Plateau down into Lake Mead. We could hear the roar of multiple falls, but we couldn't tell whether they were about to blast us off our tiny little beach into the foaming torrent or were merely distant figments of our terrified imaginations. Eventually the storm passed, and we sank into our sleeping bags, thankful to be dry and alive.

At dawn we awakened to the croak of ravens high on the wall behind our tent, the descending tremolo of canyon wrens, the quiet murmur of the river. We staggered out to discover . . . a brand new gorge. Cut through the center of our compound. Not exactly another Grand Canyon, but a gaping ravine some twelve feet wide and ten feet deep that neatly divided our tent site from the kitchen area, and that had funneled away about a third of all the horizontal real estate between the river and the cliff. Had it made its midnight course a few degrees to the right of center, some of us would not have been around this morning to enjoy the sausage and eggs, hash browns, cantaloupe, English muffins, and steaming pots of cowboy coffee.

September 25: For thrills and chills today, we have Crystal Rapid. Negotiating Crystal is an odious prospect—not only because it is dangerous, but also because in recent years it has featured so largely in every boatman's favorite pastime, the telling of river horror stories. In 1966 a flash flood in Crystal Creek washed huge boulders down into the Colorado and created what was, by most standards, a nasty rapid where there was only a riffle before. Then in 1983—the year of the floods, the year Lake Powell lapped at the top of the concrete dam impounding it—the Bureau of Reclamation opened everything it could open at Glen Canyon, and the river ran five times its normal flow, day and night, for weeks. A hundred thousand cubic feet per second. There were serious consequences to the beaches and plant life along the riparian corridor; there were serious consequences at Crystal Rapid. It got rearranged once again. It got worse than nasty.

People who ran Crystal during the flood like to reminisce (perhaps with appropriate embellishment) about the humongous hole created just below Slate Creek, a crater a hundred feet wide and thirty feet deep, with a twenty-foot standing wall of water at the bottom

Above the confluence of the Colorado and the Little Colorado, the river appears green and relatively clear, its sediment load trapped in Lake Powell by Glen Canyon Dam. When there has been no rain and the Little Colorado has been dry for a long period of time, the Colorado flows without its cargo of silt all the way to Lake Mead.

and a hydraulic force equivalent to tide rips in the Georgia Straits; they like to recall the hapless ones, the massive pontoon rigs who didn't stop to scout the rapid because they didn't know it had been altered, and anyway, with their outriggers and big motors they could always power through anything—except that this time they couldn't and went in like breaching whales, spy-hopping in the standing wave and flipping over like plastic toys in a kid's bathtub. They manufactured some of the most spectacular wrecks ever witnessed, with twenty or thirty people per boat ejected into the icy maelstrom, and gear strewn all over the river—food, garbage, port-a-pots, and all.

At least one person drowned, a lot got stranded on rocks and up against sheer cliff walls, and eventually the Department of the Interior had to bring in Navy Seals to pull people out. The only light moment occurred later during a Park Service inquiry into the whole catastrophe, when Georgie White, one of the pioneer commercial outfitters on the river, is reported to have observed about her own loss of clientele in Crystal, "They just don't make passengers like they used to. I told 'em to hang on."

But that was 1983, the flood year. Crystal has been somewhat subdued by the interim regulated flows that were instituted back in 1991, at least until the environmental studies on the impact of Glen Canyon Dam on the river's resources have been completed. From the boulder where I sit, staring for about an hour at the Colorado's worst rapid, it still looks like a nightmare, with two bodacious declivities in its carotid artery into which it seems to me one could lose a ten-ton truck. Cotton-mouthed and sniveling, I go back up to the boats and eviscerate myself cinching down my life jacket. There is no way out of this.

Ours is the second boat in line. I go into the top of the rapid along the right bank—but not so far right that I can hit the rocks poking up along the shore—power into the V-wave with a hard downstream ferry, and in order to stay right—away from those raging maws that will certainly swallow me as quickly as a toad swallows a fly—begin straining at the oars so manically I think my eyeballs may herniate . . . and slide right past both holes. Park in an eddy. Nothing to it. A piece of cake. Never even got wet. I don't know why I gave all this a moment's notice. I apologize for having built everything up so theatrically; I grovel in mortification.

September 27: We have passed from Upper Granite Gorge into Middle Granite Gorge and the Granite Narrows. The principle feature here, not surprisingly, is granite, and it can become very oppressive even when one is being cheered by the prospect of another meal. Powell's men didn't like it from the beginning, Jack Sumner reporting that "this part of the canyon is probably the worst hole in America, if not in the world. The gloomy black rocks of the Archean formation drive all the spirit out of a man."

I'm sure it is environmentally incorrect to find fault with the geological splendors of the Grand Canyon, but there are times when I find the labyrinthine walls as oppressive as

In contrast to the muddy water of the Colorado River in the main gorge, streams in the side canyons are generally crystal clear like this one at Ribbon Falls in a tributary of Bright Angel Creek.

Sumner (who had no idea where they led), and the cramped gorge conveys little more to me than a chilly reminder of my mortality. The view from the river is not so jolly as the vistas from the rim, and I often feel as if I'm at the bottom of the grave looking up. Every now and then, a cold draft blows across my sunburned shoulders. Chilled, I look around. Out of what cleft in these walls of sheer, black granite might that icy finger have come? In the ancient, two-billion-year-old schist, I make gloomy comparisons to the nanosecond of my own life.

But . . . there I go again. There are also times when I find this the most sublime piece of unreal estate on earth and can't imagine why I'd want to be anywhere else. It is common experience among river travelers to lose, about the third day out, their connection to the "normal" world—what time it is, what day, even what month. Obligations back home are forgotten, along with heretofore critical issues like who won the pennant race, when will the stock market rebound, has World War III started, is my divorce final? The house may be on fire and the children alone, but it's all a matter of supreme indifference. No phone, no fax, no E-mail, no TV, no *Wall Street Journal*. Since there is nothing to know about, there is nothing to worry about. It's a seductive state of mind. I begin to contemplate ways to make it permanent.

Then one day we drift down on Vulcan's Anvil, a towering lava rock in the river about a mile above Lava Falls. There is a niche in it on the downstream side where reverent boatmen have placed small offerings to the God of Fire, that angry deity responsible for the ordeal they are about to endure. We are gently amused to observe that it contains a condom, a half-smoked joint, and a wilted flower from the sacred datura plant.

Then it hits me—Lava Falls. LAVA FALLS! My stomach suddenly feels as if I've eaten a live rodent. The mind, what's left of it, reels. I begin to wonder whether I should ask that my body (assuming it is ever recovered) be taken up a side canyon and left for the ravens and mountain lions, or whether I really do have responsibilities back in the tangible world that demand my immediate attention, i.e., evacuation by helicopter to the Toroweap ranger station and thence by any means available across the Arizona strip to the St. George Airport. The Howlands and William Dunn abandoned Powell at Separation Rapid; wherein is it writ that I have to stay with my chums at Lava?

Let us not indulge in hyperbole. Let us simply say that Lava Falls is my personal reality check; the more I study on it, the less appealing the Grand Canyon gets, and the more I eschew the notion that it might be terribly romantic to just disappear into the southwestern landscape like some Everett Reuss redux. The "snug safety" of former ruts begins to look better and better.

Fortunately, I survive Lava Falls, even negotiate it with a certain elan. I float on down toward Diamond Creek feeling rather pleased with myself after all, my indigenous pusillanimity a fading memory, a warm spot growing again in my heart for this muddy old stream. It has carried me into the Great Unknown, and through.

And over the next few days, the canyon walls will recede, the rims drop lower, the river run quieter. The evening sky will display an even brighter bowl of stars. At the Diamond Creek take-out, we'll go about the sad but satisfying job of deflating, derigging, decompressing, deconstructing (and soon, one hopes, deodorizing). We'll head up the long, dusty trail to Peach Springs and the highway to Seligman. Where we'll hit the interstate and a time warp that will take us into Flagstaff. Where we'll soon realize that what we really want is to proceed right back up to Lees Ferry, have dinner at Marble Canyon Lodge, and launch our boats once again into the madcap unknown.

Lava Falls is an eight-second ride down a thirty-foot drop. Here, at the top, it looks benign; the bad news is about to begin.

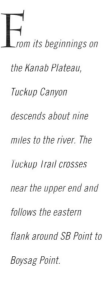

From its beginnings on the Kanab Plateau, Tuckup Canyon descends about nine miles to the river. The Tuckup Trail crosses near the upper end and follows the eastern flank around SB Point to Boysag Point.

Bright Angel Creek pools quietly at the base of granite and schist walls before emptying into the great Colorado River.

ACKNOWLEDGMENTS

There are dozens of excellent works on the Grand Canyon and its immediate environs. This book makes no claims to break new ground. It is an individual writer's impressions after almost half a century spent traveling around the Colorado Plateau by car and by foot—and, at one time or another, floating down all of its major rivers by raft. The information contained herein is general knowledge to anyone familiar with the region, and indeed, I owe a great debt to a number of experts whose work has been indispensible to me in my own research. That having been said, specialists can sometimes be pretty tough sledding, and it is my hope that the virtue of this narrative lies in an accessibility of language and style. I have tried at all times to bear in mind that the passing of information need not be a convoluted and sober affair.

The greatest debt I owe is to my father, Wallace Stegner, whose writings on the American West, as well as a lifetime of unselfish personal instruction, have kept me both informed and inspired. If there is a single book I would recommend to anyone interested in the Colorado River and the terrain through which it cuts, it is his book *Beyond the Hundredth Meridian* (Houghton Mifflin, Boston, 1954)—the story of John Wesley Powell's exploration of the Grand Canyon and the importance of that expedition in rectifying a number of misconceptions about the West and its unlimited capacity for population and development.

I am also indebted to a number of people I have known over the years who have, without always knowing it, contributed immeasurably to my understanding and appreciation of the Colorado Plateau region—in particular, Martin Litton, Rod Nash, Ann Cassidy, Alistair Blifus, Mike Walker, Dave Livermore, Chris Montague, Peter Nabokov, George Wuerthner, Ivo Lucchitta, and Jeff Garton.

Two special companions—my wife, Lynn Stegner, and my friend, Bud Bogle—have shared many river trips with me, as well as a good many hot hikes tiptoeing through the cryptogamic crust. Without them, none of this would have been any fun.

There have been so many fine books written on the Grand Canyon and the Colorado River that there is space to recommend only a few as indispensable reading. The following works have been of particular help to me in the writing of this text: Ron Redfern's *Corridors of Time*, Time Books, New York, 1980; Stephen Whitney's *A Field Guide to the Grand Canyon*, William Morrow and Company, New York, 1982; Stewart Aitchison's *A Wilderness Called Grand Canyon*, Voyager Press, Stillwater, Minnesota, 1991; Philip Fradkin's *A River No More*, Alfred A. Knopf, New York, 1981; Edmund C. Jaeger's *Desert Wildlife*, Stanford University Press, Stanford,

California, 1961; Donald Hughes's *In the House of Stone and Light: A Human History of the Grand Canyon*, Grand Canyon Natural History Association, Grand Canyon, Arizona, 1978; and Jeremy Schmidt's *Grand Canyon National Park*, Houghton Mifflin, Boston, 1993.

No study of the region should exclude Joseph Wood Krutch's *Grand Canyon, Today and All Its Yesterdays*, William Sloane Associates, New York, 1958, or Colin Fletcher's *The Man Who Walked Through Time*, Alfred A. Knopf, New York, 1967. And for those who want to get back to the most primary sources, I recommend Lieutenant Joseph C. Ives's *Report Upon the Colorado River of the West*, Office of Explorations and Surveys, Government Printing Office, Washington, DC, 1861; Clarence Dutton's *Tertiary History of the Grand Canyon District with Atlas*, U.S. Geological Survey Monographs, Volume II, Government Printing Office, Washington, D.C, 1882; and John Wesley Powell's *The Exploration of the Colorado River and Its Canyons*, Government Printing Office, Washington, DC, 1875.

PAGE STEGNER
Santa Cruz, California

Many thanks to the Grand Canyon Dories crew for sharing their intimate knowledge of the inner canyon: Moki Johnson, Bronco Bruchak, Roger Dale, Rondo Buecheler, Lee Hall, Stephanie White and B.J. Boyle, Eric Trenbeath and Donna Mehler. Thanks to Page Stegner for shared campfires, to my wife, Melissa, for her support and encouragement and to all the folks at Tehabi Books. I especially thank my father, Wayne Garton, for introducing me to the Grand Canyon twenty-three years ago.

JEFF GARTON
Tucson, Arizona

INDEX